TEACHING AS A SUBVERSIVE ACTIVITY

TEACHING AS A SUBVERSIVE ACTIVITY

Neil Postman / Charles Weingartner

A DELTA BOOK

A DELTA BOOK
Published by Dell Publishing Co., Inc.
1 Dag Hammarskjold Plaza, New York, N.Y. 10017
Copyright © 1969 by Neil Postman and Charles Weingartner
All rights reserved.
Delta ® TM 755118, Dell Publishing Co., Inc.
ISBN: 0-385-29009-8
Reprinted by arrangement with
Delacorte Press, New York, New York
Manufactured in the United States of America

Thank God there are no free schools or printing;
. . . for learning has brought disobedience and heresy
into the world, and printing has divulged them. . . .
God keep us from both.

SIR WILLIAM BERKELEY
Governor of Virginia, d. *1677*

Contents

I

What did you learn in school today,
Dear little boy of mine?
What did you learn in school today,
Dear little boy of mine?
I learned that Washington never told a lie,
I learned that soldiers seldom die,
I learned that everybody's free,
That's what the teacher said to me,
And that's what I learned in school today,
That's what I learned in school.

II

What did you learn in school today,
Dear little boy of mine?
What did you learn in school today,
Dear little boy of mine?
I learned that policemen are my friends,
I learned that justice never ends,
I learned that murderers die for their crimes,
Even if we make a mistake sometimes,
And that's what I learned in school today,
That's what I learned in school.

III

What did you learn in school today,
Dear little boy of mine?
What did you learn in school today,
Dear little boy of mine?
I learned our government must be strong,
It's always right and never wrong,
Our leaders are the finest men,
And we elect them again and again,
And that's what I learned in school today,
That's what I learned in school.

IV

What did you learn in school today,
Dear little boy of mine?
What did you learn in school today,
Dear little boy of mine?
I learned that war is not so bad,
I learned about the great ones we have had,
We fought in Germany and in France,
And someday I might get my chance,
And that's what I learned in school today,
That's what I learned in school.

Introduction

THIS BOOK is based on two assumptions of ours. One, it seems to us, is indisputable; the other, highly questionable. We refer to the beliefs that (a) in general, the survival of our society is threatened by an increasing number of unprecedented and, to date, insoluble problems; and (b) that something can be done to improve the situation. If you do not know which of these is indisputable and which questionable, you have just finished reading this book.

If you do, we do not need to document in great detail assumption (a). We do want, however, to remind you of some of the problems we currently face and then to explain briefly why we have not outgrown the hope that many of them can be minimized if not eliminated through a new approach to education.

One can begin almost anywhere in compiling a list of problems that, taken together and left unresolved, mean disaster for us and our children. For example, the number one health problem in the United States is mental illness: there are more

Americans suffering from mental illness than from all other forms of illness combined. Of almost equal magnitude is the crime problem. It is advancing rapidly on many fronts, from delinquency among affluent adolescents to frauds perpetrated by some of our richest corporations. Another is the suicide problem. Are you aware that suicide is the second most common cause of death among adolescents? Or how about the problem of "damaged" children? The most common cause of infant mortality in the United States is parental beating. Still another problem concerns misinformation—commonly referred to as "the credibility gap" or "news management." The misinformation problem takes a variety of forms, such as lies, clichés, and rumors, and implicates almost everybody, including the President of the United States.

Many of these problems are related to, or at least seriously affected by, the communications revolution, which, having taken us unawares, has ignited the civil-rights problem, unleashed the electronic-bugging problem, and made visible the sex problem, to say nothing of the drug problem. Then we have the problems stemming from the population explosion, which include the birth-control problem, the abortion problem, the housing problem, the parking problem, and the food and water-supply problem.

You may have noticed that almost all of these problems are related to "progress," a somewhat paradoxical manifestation that has also resulted in the air-pollution problem, the water-pollution problem, the garbage-disposal problem, the radio-activity problem, the megalopolis problem, the supersonic-jet-noise problem, the traffic problem, the who-am-I problem, and the what-does-it-all-mean problem.

Stay one more paragraph, for we must not omit alluding to the international scene: the Bomb problem, the Vietnam problem, the Red China problem, the Cuban problem, the Middle East problem, the foreign-aid problem, the national-defense problem, and a mountain of others mostly thought of as stemming from the communist-conspiracy problem.

Now, there is one problem under which all of the foregoing

may be subsumed. It is the "What, if anything, can we do about these problems?" problem, and *that* is exactly what this book tries to be about. This book was written because we are serious, dedicated, professional educators, which means that we are simple, romantic men who risk contributing to the mental-health problem by maintaining a belief in the improvability of the human condition through education. We are not so simple and romantic as to believe that all of the problems we have enumerated are susceptible to solution—through education or anything else. But some can be solved, and perhaps more directly through education than any other means.

School, after all, is the one institution in our society that is inflicted on everybody, and what happens in school makes a difference—for good or ill. We use the word "inflicted" because we believe that the way schools are currently conducted does very little, and quite probably nothing, to enhance our chances of mutual survival; that is, to help us solve any or even some of the problems we have mentioned. One way of representing the present condition of our educational system is as follows: It is as if we are driving a multimillion dollar sports car, screaming, "Faster! Faster!" while peering fixedly into the rearview mirror. It is an awkward way to try to tell where we are, much less where we are going, and it has been sheer dumb luck that we have not smashed ourselves to bits— so far. We have paid almost exclusive attention to the car, equipping it with all sorts of fantastic gadgets and an engine that will propel it at ever increasing speeds, but we seem to have forgotten where we wanted to go in it. Obviously, we are in for a helluva jolt. The question is not whether, but when.

It is the thesis of this book that change—constant, accelerating, ubiquitous—is the most striking characteristic of the world we live in and that our educational system has not yet recognized this fact. We maintain, further, that the abilities and attitudes required to deal adequately with change are those of the highest priority and that it is not beyond our ingenuity to design school environments which can help young people to master concepts necessary to survival in a rapidly changing world. The institution we call "school" is what it is because we made it that way. If it is irrelevant, as Marshall McLuhan says; if it shields children from reality, as Norbert Wiener says; if it educates for obsolescence, as John Gardner says; if it does not develop intelligence, as Jerome Bruner says; if it is based on fear, as John Holt says; if it avoids the promotion of significant learnings, as Carl Rogers says; if it induces alienation, as Paul Goodman says; if it punishes creativity and independence, as Edgar Friedenberg says; if, in short, it is not doing what needs to be done, it can be changed; it *must* be changed. It can be changed, we believe, because there are so many wise men who, in one way or another, have offered us clear, intelligent, and new ideas to use, and as long as these ideas and the alternatives they suggest are available, there is no reason to abandon hope. We have mentioned some of these men above. We will allude to, explicate, or otherwise use the ideas of still others throughout this book. For example, Alfred Korzybski, I. A. Richards, Adelbert Ames, Earl Kelley, Alan Watts.

All of these men have several things in common. They are almost all "romantics," which is to say they believe that the human situation is improvable through intelligent innovation. They are all courageous and imaginative thinkers, which means they are beyond the constricting intimidation of conventional assumptions. They all have tried to deal with contemporary problems, which means they can tell the difference between an irrelevant, dead idea and a relevant, viable one. And finally, most of them are not usually thought of as educators. This last is extremely important, since it reveals another critical assumption of ours: namely, that within the "Educational Establishment" there are insufficient daring and vigorous ideas on which to build a new approach to education. One must look to men whose books would rarely be used, or even thought of, in education courses, and would not be listed under the subject "Education" in libraries.

So, whatever else its shortcomings, this book will be different from most other books on education. It was not our intention to be different. It just worked out that way because there are so few men currently working as professional educators who have anything germane to say about changing our educational system to fit present realities. Almost all of them deal with qualitative problems in quantitative terms, and, in doing so, miss the point. The fact is that our present educational system is not viable and is certainly not capable of generating enough energy to lead to its own revitalization. What is needed is a kind of shock therapy with stimulation supplied by other, living sources. And this is what we try to do. For us, McLuhan's *Understanding Media*, Wiener's *The Human Use of Human Beings*, Rogers' *On Becoming a Person*, Korzybski's *Science and Sanity*, even Richards' *Practical Criticism* (to name a few) are such sources. In other words, they are "education" books, and, in our opinion, the best kind. We mean by this that these books not only present ideas that are relevant to current reality but that the ideas suggest an entirely different and more relevant conception of education than our schools have so far managed to reflect. This is an education that develops in youth a competence in applying the best available strategies for survival in a world filled with unprecedented troubles, uncertainties, and opportunities. Our task, then, is to make these strategies for survival visible and explicit in the hope that someone somewhere will act on them.

NEIL POSTMAN
CHARLES WEINGARTNER

New York, 1968

TEACHING AS
A SUBVERSIVE
ACTIVITY

TEACHING AS
A SUBVERSIVE ACTIVITY

NOTICE

Please be advised that page 61 of this book
has been left blank deliberately,
as explained in the first line of page 60.

I. Crap Detecting

"IN 1492, COLUMBUS DISCOVERED AMERICA. . . ." Starting
from this disputed fact, each one of us will describe the history
of this country in a somewhat different way. Nonetheless, it
is reasonable to assume that most of us would include something about what is called the "democratic process," and how
Americans have valued it, or at least have said they valued it.
Therein lies a problem: one of the tenets of a democratic
society is that men be allowed to think and express themselves
freely on any subject, even to the point of speaking out against
the idea of a democratic society. To the extent that our schools
are instruments of such a society, they must develop in the
young not only an awareness of this freedom but a will to
exercise it, and the intellectual power and perspective to do
so effectively. This is necessary so that the society may continue to change and modify itself to meet unforeseen threats,
problems, and opportunities. Thus, we can achieve what John
Gardner calls an "ever-renewing society."

So goes the theory.

1

In practice, we mostly get a different story. In our society, as in others, we find that there are influential men at the head of important institutions who cannot afford to be found wrong, who find change inconvenient, perhaps intolerable, and who have financial or political interests they must conserve at any cost. Such men are, therefore, threatened in many respects by the theory of the democratic process and the concept of an ever-renewing society. Moreover, we find that there are obscure men who do *not* head important institutions who are similarly threatened because they have identified themselves with certain ideas and institutions which they wish to keep free from either criticism or change.

Such men as these would much prefer that the schools do little or nothing to encourage youth to question, doubt, or challenge any part of the society in which they live, especially those parts which are most vulnerable. "After all," say the practical men, "they are *our* schools, and they ought to promote *our* interests, and *that* is part of the democratic process, too." True enough; and here we have a serious point of conflict. Whose schools are they, anyway, and whose interests should they be designed to serve? We realize that these are questions about which any self-respecting professor of education could write several books, each one beginning with a reminder that the problem is not black or white, either/or, yes or no. But if you have read our introduction, you will not expect us to be either professorial or prudent. We are, after all, trying to suggest strategies for survival as they may be developed in our schools, and the situation requires emphatic responses. We believe that the schools must serve as the principal medium for developing in youth the attitudes and skills of social, political, and cultural criticism. No. That is not emphatic enough. Try this: In the early 1960s, an interviewer was trying to get Ernest Hemingway to identify the characteristics required for a person to be a "great writer." As the interviewer offered a list of various possibilities, Hemingway disparaged each in sequence. Finally, frustrated, the interviewer asked, "Isn't there any one essential ingredient that you can identify?" Hemingway replied, "Yes, there is. In order to be a great writer a person must have a built-in, shockproof crap detector."

It seems to us that, in his response, Hemingway identified an essential survival strategy and the essential function of the schools in today's world. One way of looking at the history of the human group is that it has been a continuing struggle against the veneration of "crap." Our intellectual history is a chronicle of the anguish and suffering of men who tried to help their contemporaries see that some part of their fondest beliefs were misconceptions, faulty assumptions, superstitions, and even outright lies. The mileposts along the road of our intellectual development signal those points at which some person developed a new perspective, a new meaning, or a new metaphor. We have in mind a new education that would set out to cultivate just such people—experts at "crap detecting."

There are many ways of describing this function of the schools, and many men who have. David Riesman, for example, calls this the "counter-cyclical" approach to education, meaning that schools should stress values that are not stressed by other major institutions in the culture. Norbert Wiener insisted that the schools now must function as "anti-entropic feedback systems," "entropy" being the word used to denote a general and unmistakable tendency of all systems—natural and man-made—in the universe to "run down," to reduce to chaos and uselessness. This is a process that cannot be reversed but that can be slowed down and partly controlled. One way to control it is through "maintenance." This is Eric Hoffer's term, and he believes that the quality of maintenance is one of the best indices of the quality of life in a culture. But Wiener uses a different metaphor to get at the same idea. He says that in order for there to be an anti-entropic force, we must have adequate feedback. In other words, we must have instruments to tell us when we are running down, when maintenance is required. For Wiener, such instruments would be people who have been educated to recognize change, to be sensitive to problems caused by change, and who have the motivation and courage to sound alarms when entropy accelerates to a dangerous degree. This is what we mean by "crap detecting." It is also what John Gardner means by the "ever-renewing society," and what Kenneth Boulding means by "social self-consciousness." We are talking about the schools' cultivating in the young that most "subversive" intellectual instrument—the anthropological perspective. This perspective allows one to be part of his own culture and, at the same time, to be out of it. One views the activities of his own group as would an anthropologist, observing its tribal rituals, its fears, its conceits, its ethnocentrism. In this way, one is able to recognize when reality begins to drift too far away from the grasp of the tribe.

We need hardly say that achieving such a perspective is extremely difficult, requiring, among other things, considerable courage. We are, after all, talking about achieving a high degree of freedom from the intellectual and social constraints of one's tribe. For example, it is generally assumed that people of other tribes have been victimized by indoctrination from which our tribe has remained free. Our own outlook seems "natural" to us, and we wonder that other men can perversely persist in believing nonsense. Yet, it is undoubtedly true that, for most people, the acceptance of a particular doctrine is largely attributable to the accident of birth. They might be said to be "ideologically interchangeable," which means that they would have accepted any set of doctrines that happened to be valued by the tribe to which they were born. Each of us, whether from the American tribe, Russian tribe, or Hopi tribe, is born into a symbolic environment as well as a physical one. We become accustomed very early to a "natural" way of talking, and being talked to, about "truth." Quite arbitrarily, one's perception of what is "true" or real is shaped by the symbols and symbol-manipulating institutions of his tribe. Most men, in time, learn to respond with fervor and obedience to a set of verbal abstractions which they feel provides them with an ideological identity. One word for this, of course, is "prejudice." None of us is free of it, but it is the sign of a competent "crap detector" that he is not completely captivated by the arbitrary abstractions of the community in which he happened to grow up.

In our own society, if one grows up in a language environment which includes and approves such a concept as "white supremacy," one can quite "mor? ly" engage in the process of murdering civil-rights workers. Similarly, if one is living in a language environment where the term "black power" crystalizes an ideological identity, one can engage, again quite "morally," in acts of violence against any nonblack persons or their property. An insensitivity to the unconscious effects of our "natural" metaphors condemns us to highly constricted perceptions of how things are and, therefore, to highly limited alternative modes of behavior.

Those who *are* sensitive to the verbally built-in biases of their "natural" environment seem "subversive" to those who are not. There is probably nothing more dangerous to the prejudices of the latter than a man in the process of discovering that the language of his group is limited, misleading, or one-sided. Such a man is dangerous because he is not easily enlisted on the side of one ideology or another, because he sees beyond the words to the processes which give an ideology its reality. In his *May Man Prevail?*, Erich Fromm gives us an example of a man (himself) in the process of doing just that:

> The Russians believe that they represent socialism because they talk in terms of Marxist ideology, and they do not recognize how similar their system is to the most developed form of capitalism. We in the West believe that we represent the system of individualism, private initiative, and humanistic ethics, because we hold on to *our* ideology, and we do not see that our institutions have, in fact, in many ways become more and more similar to the hated system of communism.

Religious indoctrination is still another example of this point. As Alan Watts has noted: "Irrevocable commitment to any religion is not only intellectual suicide; it is positive unfaith because it closes the mind to any new vision of the world.

Faith is, above all, openness—an act of trust in the unknown."
And so "crap detecting" requires a perspective on what Watts
calls "the standard-brand religions." That perspective can also
be applied to knowledge. If you substitute the phrase "set of
facts" for the word "religion" in the quotation above, the statement is equally important and accurate.

The need for this kind of perspective has always been urgent
but never so urgent as now. We will not take you again
through that painful catalogue of twentieth-century problems
we cited in our Introduction. There are, however, three particular problems which force us to conclude that the schools
must consciously remake themselves into training centers for
"subversion." In one sense, they are all one problem but for
purposes of focus may be distinguished from each other.

The first goes under the name of the "communications revolution," or media change. As Father John Culkin of Fordham
University likes to say, a lot of things have happened in this
century and most of them plug into walls. To get some perspective on the electronic plug, imagine that your home and
all the other homes and buildings in your neighborhood have
been cordoned off, and from them will be removed all the
electric and electronic inventions that have appeared in the
last 50 years. The media will be substracted in reverse order,
with the most recent going first. The first thing to leave your
house, then, is the television set—and everybody will stand
there as if they are attending the funeral of a friend, wonder-
ing, "What are we going to do tonight?" After rearranging the
furniture so that it is no longer aimed at a blank space in the
room, you suggest going to the movies. But there won't be any.
Nor will there be LP records, tapes, radio, telephone, or telegraph. If you are thinking that the absence of the media would
only affect your entertainment and information, remember
that, at some point, your electric lights would be removed,
and your refrigerator, and your heating system, and your air
conditioner. In short, you would have to be a totally different
person from what you are in order to survive for more than
a day. The chances are slim that you could modify yourself

and your patterns of living and believing fast enough to save yourself. As you were expiring, you would at least know something about how it was before the electric plug. Or perhaps you wouldn't. In any case, if you had energy and interest enough to hear him, any good ecologist could inform you of the logic of your problem: a change in an environment is rarely only additive or linear. You seldom, if ever, have an old environment *plus* a new element, such as a printing press or an electric plug. *What you have is a totally new environment requiring a whole new repertoire of survival strategies.* In no case is this more certain than when the new elements are technological. Then, in no case will the new environment be more radically different from the old than in political and social forms of life. When you plug something into a wall, someone is getting plugged into you. Which means you need new patterns of defense, perception, understanding, evaluation. You need a new kind of education.

It was George Counts who observed that technology repealed the Bill of Rights. In the eighteenth century, a pamphlet could influence an entire nation. Today all the ideas of the Noam Chomskys, Paul Goodmans, Edgar Friedenbergs, I. F. Stones, and even the William Buckleys, cannot command as much attention as a 30-minute broadcast by Walter Cronkite. Unless, of course, one of them were given a prime-time network program, in which case he would most likely come out more like Walter Cronkite than himself. Even Marshall McLuhan, who is leading the field in understanding media, is having his ideas transformed and truncated by the forms of the media to fit present media functions. (One requirement, for example, is that an idea or a man must be "sensational" in order to get a hearing; thus, McLuhan comes out not as a scholar studying media but as the "Apostle of the Electronic Age.")

We trust it is clear that we are not making the typical, whimpering academic attack on the media. We are not "against" the media. Any more, incidentally, than McLuhan is "for" the media. You cannot reverse technological change.

Things that plug in are here to stay. But you can study media, with a view toward discovering what they are doing to you. As McLuhan has said, there is no inevitability so long as there is a willingness to contemplate what is happening.

Very few of us have contemplated more rigorously what is happening through media change than Jacques Ellul, who has sounded some chilling alarms. Without mass media, Ellul insists, there can be no effective propaganda. With them, there is almost nothing but. "Only through concentration of a large number of media in a few hands can one attain a true orchestration, a continuity, and an application of scientific methods of influencing individuals." That such concentration is occurring daily, Ellul says, is an established fact, and its results may well be an almost total homogenization of thought among those the media reach. We cannot afford to ignore Norbert Wiener's observation of a paradox that results from our increasing technological capability in electronic communication: as the number of messages increases, the amount of information carried decreases. We have more media to communicate   · fewer significant ideas.

Still another way of saying this is that, while there has been a tremendous increase in media, there has been, at the same time, a decrease in available and viable "democratic" channels of communication because the mass media are entirely one-way communication. For example, as a means of affecting public policy, the town meeting is dead. Significant community action (without violence) is increasingly rare. A small printing press in one's home, as an instrument of social change, is absurd. Traditional forms of dissent and protest seem impractical, e.g., letters to the editor, street-corner speeches, etc. No one can reach many people unless he has access to the mass media. As this is written, for example, there is no operational two-way communication possible with respect to United States policies and procedures in Vietnam. The communication is virtually all one way: from the top down, via the mass media, especially TV. The pressure on everyone is to subscribe without question to policies formulated in the Pentagon. The

President appears on TV and clearly makes the point that any-one who does not accept "our policy" can be viewed only as lending aid and comfort to the enemy. The position has been elaborately developed in all media that "peaceniks" are failing in the obligation to "support our boys overseas." The effect of this process on all of us is to leave no alternative but to accept policy, act on orders from above, and implement the policy without question or dialogue. This is what Edgar Friedenberg calls "creeping Eichmannism," a sort of spiritless, mechanical, abstract functioning which does not allow much room for in-dividual thought and action.

As Paul Goodman has pointed out, there are many forms of censorship, and one of them is to deny access to "loudspeakers" to those with dissident ideas, or even *any* ideas. This is easy to do (and not necessarily conspiratorial) when the loudspeakers are owned and operated by mammoth corporations with enor-mous investments in their proprietorship. What we get is an entirely new politics, including the possibility that a major requirement for the holding of political office be prior success as a show-business personality. Goodman writes in *Like a Conquered Province:*

> The traditional American sentiment is that a decent society cannot be built by dominant official policy anyway, but only by grassroots resistance, community cooperation, individual enterprise, and citizenly vigilance to protect liberty. . . . *The question is whether or not our beautiful libertarian, pluralist, and populist experiment is viable in modern conditions.* If it's not, I don't know any other acceptable politics, and I am a man without a country.

Is it possible that there are millions becoming men without a country? Men who are increasingly removed from the sources of power? Men who have fewer and fewer ideas available to them, and fewer and fewer ways of expressing themselves meaningfully and effectively? Might the frustration thus en-gendered be one of the causes of the increasing use of violence as a form of statement?

We come then to a second problem which makes necessary a "subversive" role for the schools. This one may appropriately be called the "Change Revolution." In order to illustrate what this means, we will use the media again and the metaphor of a clock face. Imagine a clock face with 60 minutes on it. Let the clock stand for the time men have had access to writing systems. Our clock would thus represent something like 3,000 years, and each minute on our clock 50 years. On this scale, there were no significant media changes until about nine minutes ago. At that time, the printing press came into use in Western culture. About three minutes ago, the telegraph, photograph, and locomotive arrived. Two minutes ago: the telephone, rotary press, motion pictures, automobile, airplane, and radio. One minute ago, the talking picture. Television has appeared in the last ten seconds, the computer in the last five, and communications satellites in the last second. The laser beam—perhaps the most potent medium of communication of all—appeared only a fraction of a second ago.

It would be possible to place almost any area of life on our clock face and get roughly the same measurements. For example, in medicine, you would have almost no significant changes until about one minute ago. In fact, until one minute ago, as Jerome Frank has said, almost the whole history of medicine is the history of the placebo effect. About a minute ago, antibiotics arrived. About ten seconds ago, open-heart surgery. In fact, within the past ten seconds there probably have been more changes in medicine than is represented by all the rest of the time on our clock. This is what some people call the "knowledge explosion." It is happening in every field of knowledge susceptible to scientific inquiry.

The standard reply to any comment about change (for example, from many educators) is that change isn't new and that it is easy to exaggerate its meaning. To such replies, Norbert Wiener had a useful answer: the difference between a fatal and a therapeutic dose of strychnine is "only a matter of degree." In other words, change isn't new; what is new is the *degree of change*. As our clock-face metaphor was intended to suggest, about three minutes ago there developed a qualitative difference in the character of change. Change changed.

This is really quite a new problem. For example, up until the last generation it was possible to be born, grow up, and spend a life in the United States without moving more than 50 miles from home, without ever confronting serious questions about one's basic values, beliefs, and patterns of behavior. Indeed, without ever confronting serious challenges to anything one knew. Stability and consequent predictability—within "natural cycles"—was the characteristic mode. But now, in just the last minute, we've reached the stage where change occurs so rapidly that each of us in the course of our lives has continuously to work out a set of values, beliefs, and patterns of behavior that are viable, or *seem* viable, to each of us personally. And just when we have identified a workable system, it turns out to be irrelevant because so much has changed while we were doing it.

Of course, this frustrating state of affairs applies to our education as well. If you are over twenty-five years of age, the mathematics you were taught in school is "old"; the grammar you were taught is obsolete and in disrepute; the biology, completely out of date, and the history, open to serious question. The best that can be said of you, assuming that you *remember* most of what you were told and read, is that you are a walking encyclopedia of outdated information. As Alfred North Whitehead pointed out in *The Adventure of Ideas:*

> Our sociological theories, our political philosophy, our practical maxims of business, our political economy, and our doctrines of education are derived from an unbroken tradition of great thinkers and of practical examples from the age of Plato . . . to the end of the last century. The whole of this tradition is warped by the vicious assumption that each generation will substantially live amid the conditions governing the lives of its fathers and will transmit those conditions to mould with equal force the lives of its children. *We are living in the first period of human history for which this assumption is false.*

All of which brings us to the third problem: the "burgeoning bureaucracy." We are brought there because bureaucracies, in spite of their seeming indispensability, are by their nature highly resistant to change. The motto of most bureaucracies is, "Carry On, Regardless." There is an essential mindlessness about them which causes them, in most circumstances, to accelerate entropy rather than to impede it. Bureaucracies rarely ask themselves Why?, but only How? John Gardner, who as President of the Carnegie Corporation and (as of this writing) Secretary of Health, Education, and Welfare has learned about bureaucracies at first hand, has explained them very well:

> To accomplish renewal, we need to understand what prevents it. When we talk about revitalizing a society, we tend to put exclusive emphasis on finding new ideas. But there is usually no shortage of new ideas; the problem is to get · a hearing for them. And that means breaking through the crusty rigidity and stubborn complacency of the *status quo.* The aging society develops elaborate defenses against new ideas— "mind-forged manacles," in William Blake's vivid phrase. . . . As a society becomes more concerned with precedent and custom, it comes to care more about how things are done and less about *whether* they are done. The man who wins acclaim is not the one who "gets things done" but the one who has an ingrained knowledge of the rules and accepted practices. Whether he accomplishes anything is less important than whether he conducts himself in an "appropriate" manner.
>
> The body of custom, convention, and "reputable" standards exercises such an oppressive effect on creative minds that new developments in a field often originate outside the area of respectable practice.

In other words, bureaucracies are the repositories of conventional assumptions and standard practices—two of the greatest accelerators of entropy.

We could put before you a volume of other quotations—from Machiavelli to Paul Goodman—describing how bureaucratic structures retard the development and application of new survival strategies. But in doing so, we would risk creating the impression that we stand with Goodman in yearning for some anarchistic Utopia in which the Army, the Police, General Motors, the U.S. Office of Education, the Post Office, et al. do not exist. We are not "against" bureaucracies, any more than we are "for" them. They are like electric plugs. They will probably not go away, but they do need to be controlled if the prerogatives of a democratic society are to remain visible and usable. This is why we ask that the schools be "subversive," that they serve as a kind of antibureaucracy bureaucracy, providing the young with a "What is it good for?" perspective on its own society. Certainly, it is unrealistic to expect those who control the media to perform that function. Nor the generals and the politicians. Nor is it reasonable to expect the "intellectuals" to do it, for they do not have access to the majority of youth. But schoolteachers do, and so the primary responsibility rests with them.

The trouble is that most teachers have the idea that they are in some other sort of business. Some believe, for example, that they are in the "information dissemination" business. This was a reasonable business up to about a minute or two ago on our clock. (But then, so was the horseshoe business and the candle-snuffer business.) The signs that their business is failing are abundant, but they keep at it all the more diligently. Santayana told us that a fanatic is someone who redoubles his efforts when he has forgotten his aim. In this case, even if the aim has not been forgotten, it is simply irrelevant. But the effort has been redoubled anyway.

There are some teachers who think they are in the "transmission of our cultural heritage" business, which is not an unreasonable business if you are concerned with the whole clock and not just its first 57 minutes. The trouble is that most teachers find the last three minutes too distressing to deal with, which is exactly why they are in the wrong business. Their students find the last three minutes distressing—and confusing —too, especially the last 30 seconds, and they need *help*. While they have to live with TV, film, the LP record, communication satellites, and the laser beam, their teachers are still talking as if the only medium on the scene is Gutenberg's printing press. While they have to understand psychology and psychedelics, anthropology and anthropomorphism, birth control and biochemistry, their teachers are teaching "subjects" that mostly don't exist anymore. While they need to find new roles for themselves as social, political, and religious organisms, their teachers (as Edgar Friedenberg has documented so painfully) are acting almost entirely as shills for corporate interests, shaping them up to be functionaries in one bureaucracy or another.

Unless our schools can switch to the right business, their clientele will either go elsewhere (as many are doing) or go into a severe case of "future shock," to use a relatively new phrase. Future shock occurs when you are confronted by the fact that the world you were educated to believe in doesn't exist. Your images of reality are apparitions that disappear on contact. There are several ways of responding to such a condition, one of which is to withdraw and allow oneself to be overcome by a sense of impotence. More commonly, one continues to act *as if* his apparitions were substantial, relentlessly pursuing a course of action that he knows will fail him. You may have noticed that there are scores of political, social, and religious leaders who are clearly suffering from advanced cases of future shock. They repeat over and over again the words that are supposed to represent the world about them. But nothing seems to work out. And then they repeat the words again and again. Alfred Korzybski used a somewhat different metaphor to describe what we have been calling "future shock." He likened one's language to a map. The map is intended to describe the territory that we call "reality," i.e., the world outside of our skins. When there is a close correspondence between map and territory, there tends to be a high degree of effective functioning, especially where it relates to survival. When there is little correspondence between map and territory, there is a strong tendency for entropy to make substantial gains. In this context, the terrifying question What did you learn in school today? assumes immense importance for all of us. We just may not survive another generation of inadvertent entropy helpers.

What is the necessary business of the schools? To create eager consumers? To transmit the dead ideas, values, metaphors, and information of three minutes ago? To create smoothly functioning bureaucrats? *These* aims are truly subversive since they undermine our chances of surviving as a viable, democratic society. And they do their work in the name of convention and standard practice. We would like to see the schools go into the anti-entropy business. Now, that is subversive, too. But the purpose is to subvert attitudes, beliefs, and assumptions that foster chaos and uselessness.

II. The Medium Is the Message, Of Course

ONE OF THE MOST DANGEROUS MEN around at the moment—dangerous because he seems to be subverting traditional assumptions—is Marshall McLuhan. Nonetheless, as of this writing he is capturing the attention of intellectuals and the press as few educationists have ever done. One of the reasons is the seeming uniqueness of his remarks. Another is the unconventional manner in which he conducts his reflections. And a third is that he is not generally thought of as an educationist. If he were, he would probably lose a sizable portion of his audience. Nobody likes a smart educationist. Or at least nobody wants to be counted among his listeners. That is why Jerome Bruner insists on being called a psychologist and Edgar Friedenberg, a sociologist.

But McLuhan is an operational educationist nonetheless. Moreover, some of his "probings," as he calls them, are unique mostly in their metaphorical verve. (For an educationist, he expresses himself in an uncommon flow of puns and poetry.) Many of his observations are reaffirmations of ideas previously expressed by other educationists—for example, John Dewey and A. N. Whitehead—ideas which were, and still are, largely ignored by those who could most profit by them. We are especially in McLuhan's .debt for his restatement, in alliterative language, of Dewey's belief that "we learn what we do." McLuhan means much the same thing by his famous aphorism, "The medium is the message" (which for emphasis, fun, and publicity he has rephrased, "The medium is the massage"). From this perspective, one is invited to see that the most important impressions made on a human nervous system come from the character and structure of the environment within which the nervous system functions; that the environment itself conveys the critical and dominant messages by controlling the perceptions and attitudes of those who participate in it. Dewey stressed that the role an individual is assigned in an environment—what he is permitted to do—is what the individual learns. In other words, the medium itself, i.e., the environment, is the message. "Message" here means the perceptions you are allowed to build, the attitudes you are enticed to assume, the sensitivities you are encouraged to develop— almost all of the things you learn to see and feel and value. You learn them because your environment is organized in such a way that it permits or encourages or insists that you learn them.

McLuhan seems to have his most difficult moments trying to persuade his audiences that a television set or a newspaper or an automobile or a Xerox machine can usefully be defined as such an environment. And even when his audiences suspend disbelief long enough to probe with him further, McLuhan still must labor to persuade that the relevant question to ask of such environments is not "What's on TV?" or "What's in the newspaper?" but "In what ways does the structure or process of the medium-environment manipulate our senses and attitudes?"

One would think it is much easier to persuade an audience that a classroom is an environment and that the way it is organized carries the burden of what people will learn from it. Yet, oddly, it isn't. Educational discourse, especially among the educated, is so laden with preconceptions that it is practically impossible to introduce an idea that does not fit into traditional categories.

Consider as a primary case in point the notion that a classroom lesson is largely made up of two components: content and method. The content may be trivial or important, but it is always thought to be the "substance" of the lesson; it is what the students are there to "get"; it is what they are supposed to learn; it is what is "covered." Content, as any syllabus proves, exists independently of and prior to the student, and is indifferent to the media by which it is "transmitted." Method, on the other hand, is "merely" the manner in which the content is presented. The method may be imaginative or dull, but it is never more than a means of conveying the content. It has no content of its own. While it may induce excitement or boredom, it carries no message—at least none that would be asked about on the College Boards, which is to say, worthy of comment.

To our knowledge, all schools of education and teacher-training institutions in the United States are organized around the idea that content and method are separate in the manner we have described. Perhaps the most important message thus communicated to teachers in training is that this separation is real, useful, and urgent, and that it ought to be maintained in the schools. A secondary message is that, while the "content" and "method" are separate, they are not equal. Everyone knows that the "real" courses are the content courses, the kind of which James Bryant Conant is so fond: The Heritage of Greece and Rome, Calculus, Elizabethan Drama, The Civil War. The "fake" courses are the methods courses, those conspiracies of emptiness which are universally ridiculed because their finest ambition is to instruct in how to write lesson plans, when to use an overhead projector, and why it is desirable to keep the room at a comfortable temperature. (The educationists have got what they deserve on this one. Since they have saddled themselves with a trivial definition of "method," what they have been able to do in their courses has wavered from embarrassing to shocking. The professors of the liberal arts have, so far, escaped the censure and ridicule *they* deserve for not having noticed that a "discipline" or a "subject" is a way of knowing something—in other words, a method—and that, therefore, their courses are methods courses.)

"The medium is the message" implies that the invention of a dichotomy between content and method is both naïve and dangerous. *It implies that the critical content of any learning experience is the method or process through which the learning occurs.* Almost any sensible parent knows this, as does any effective top sergeant. It is not what you say to people that counts; it is what you have them *do*. If most teachers have not yet grasped this idea, it is not for lack of evidence. It may, however, be due to their failure to look in the direction where the evidence can be seen. In order to understand what kinds of behaviors classrooms promote, one must become accustomed to observing what, in fact, students actually *do* in them. What students do in the classroom is what they learn (as Dewey would say), and what they learn to do is the classroom's message (as McLuhan would say). Now, what is it that students *do* in the classroom? Well, mostly, they sit and listen to the teacher. Mostly, they are required to believe in authorities, or at least pretend to such belief when they take tests. Mostly, they are required to *remember*. They are almost never required to make observations, formulate definitions, or perform any intellectual operations that go beyond repeating what someone else says is true. They are rarely encouraged to ask substantive questions, although they are permitted to ask about administrative and technical details. (How long should the paper be? Does spelling count? When is the assignment due?) It is practically unheard of for students to play any role in determining what problems are worth studying or what procedures of inquiry ought to be used. Examine the types of questions teachers ask in classrooms, and you will find that most of them are what might technically be called "convergent questions," but which might more simply be called "Guess what I'm thinking" questions. Here are a few that will sound familiar:

> What is a noun?
> What were the three causes of the Civil War?
> What is the principal river of Uruguay?
> What is the definition of a nonrestrictive clause?
> What is the real meaning of this poem?
> How many sets of chromosomes do human beings have?
> Why did Brutus betray Caesar?

So, what students mostly do in class is guess what the teacher wants them to say. Constantly, they must try to supply "The Right Answer." It does not seem to matter if the subject is English or history or science; mostly, students *do* the same thing. And since it is indisputably (if not publicly) recognized that the ostensible "content" of such courses is rarely remembered beyond the last quiz (in which you are required to remember only 65 percent of what you were told), it is safe to say that just about the *only* learning that occurs in classrooms is that which is communicated by the structure of the classroom itself. What are these learnings? What are these messages? Here are a few among many, none of which you will ever find officially listed among the aims of teachers:

> Passive acceptance is a more desirable response to ideas than active criticism.
> Discovering knowledge is beyond the power of students and is, in any case, none of their business.
> Recall is the highest form of intellectual achievement, and the collection of unrelated "facts" is the goal of education.
> The voice of authority is to be trusted and valued more than independent judgment.
> One's own ideas and those of one's classmates are inconsequential.
> Feelings are irrelevant in education.

There is always a single, unambiguous Right Answer to a question.

English is not History and History is not Science and Science is not Art and Art is not Music, and Art and Music are minor subjects and English, History and Science major subjects, and a subject is something you "take" and, when you have taken it, you have "had" it, and if you have "had" it, you are immune and need not take it again. (The Vaccination Theory of Education?)

Each of these learnings is expressed in specific behaviors that are on constant display throughout our culture. Take, for example, the message that recall—particularly the recall of random facts—is the highest form of intellectual achievement. This belief explains the enormous popularity of quiz shows, the genuine admiration given by audiences to contestants who in 30 seconds can name the concert halls in which each of Beethoven's symphonies had its first public performance. How else explain the great delight so many take in playing Trivia? Is there a man more prized among men than he who can settle a baseball dispute by identifying without equivocation the winner of the National League RBI title in 1943? (Bill "Swish" Nicholson.)

Recently we attended a party at which the game Trivia was played. One young man sat sullen and silent through several rounds, perhaps thinking that nothing could be more dull. At some point, the question arose, "What were the names of the actor and actress who starred in *Mr. First Nighter?*" From somewhere deep within him an answer formed, and he quite astonished himself, and everyone else, by blurting it out. (Les Tremaine and Barbara Luddy.) For several moments afterward, he could not conceal his delight. He was in the fifth grade again, and the question might have been, "What is the principal river of Uruguay?" He had supplied the answer, and faster than anyone else. And that is good, as every classroom environment he'd ever been in had taught him.

Watch a man—say, a politician—being interviewed on television, and you are observing a demonstration of what both he and his interrogators learned in school: all questions have answers, and it is a good thing to give an answer even if there is none to give, even if you don't understand the question, even if the question contains erroneous assumptions, even if you are ignorant of the facts required to answer. Have you ever heard a man being interviewed say, "I don't have the faintest idea," or "I don't know enough even to guess," or "I have been asked that question before, but all my answers to it seem to be wrong?" One does not "blame" men, especially if they are politicians, for providing instant answers to all questions. The public requires that they do, since the public has learned that instant answer giving is the most important sign of an educated man.

What all of us have learned (and how difficult it is to unlearn it!) is that it is not important that our utterances satisfy the demands of the question (or of reality), but that they satisfy the demands of the classroom environment. Teacher asks. Student answers. Have you ever heard of a student who replied to a question, "Does *anyone* know the answer to that question?" or "I don't understand what I would have to do in order to find an answer," or "I have been asked that question before and, frankly, I've never understood what it meant"? Such behavior would invariably result in some form of penalty and is, of course, scrupulously avoided, except by "wise guys." Thus, students learn not to value it. They get the message. And yet few teachers consciously articulate such a message. It is not part of the "content" of their instruction. No teacher ever said: "Don't value uncertainty and tentativeness. Don't question questions. Above all, don't think." The message is communicated quietly, insidiously, relentlessly, and effectively through the structure of the classroom: through the role of the teacher, the role of the student, the rules of their verbal game, the rights that are assigned, the arrangements made for communication, the "doings" that are praised or censured. In other words, the medium is the message.

Have you ever heard of a student taking notes on the remarks of another student? Probably not. Because the organization of the classroom makes it clear that what students say is not the "content" of instruction. Therefore, it will not be included on tests. Therefore, they can ignore it.

Have you ever heard of a student indicating an interest in how a textbook writer arrived at his conclusions? Rarely, we would guess. Most students seem unaware that textbooks are written by human beings. Besides, the classroom structure does not suggest that the processes of inquiry are of any importance.

Have you ever heard of a student suggesting a more useful definition of something that the teacher has already defined? Or of a student who asked, "Whose facts are those?" Or of a student who asked, "What is a fact?" Or of a student who asked, "Why are we doing this work?"

Now, if you reflect on the fact that most classroom environments are managed so that such questions as these will not be asked, you can become very depressed. Consider, for example, where "knowledge" comes from. It isn't just *there* in a book, waiting for someone to come along and "learn" it. Knowledge is produced in response to questions. And new knowledge results from the asking of new questions; quite often new questions about old questions. Here is the point: *Once you have learned how to ask questions—relevant and appropriate and substantial questions—you have learned how to learn and no one can keep you from learning whatever you want or need to know.* Let us remind you, for a moment, of the process that characterizes school environments: what students are restricted to (solely and even vengefully) is the process of memorizing (partially and temporarily) somebody else's answers to somebody else's questions. It is staggering to consider the implications of this fact. The most important intellectual ability man has yet developed—the art and science of asking questions—is not taught in school! Moreover, it is *not* "taught" in the most devastating way possible: by arranging the environment so that significant question asking is not valued. It is doubtful if you can think of many schools that include question asking, or methods of inquiry, as part of their curriculum. But even if you knew a hundred that did, there would be little cause for celebration unless the classrooms were arranged so that students could *do* question asking; not talk about it, read about it, be told about it. Asking questions is behavior. If you don't do it, you don't learn it. It really is as simple as that.

If you go through the daily papers and listen attentively to the radio and watch television carefully, you should have no trouble perceiving that our political and social lives are conducted, to a very considerable extent, by people whose behaviors are almost precisely the behaviors their school environments demanded of them. We do not need to document for you the pervasiveness of dogmatism and intellectual timidity, the fear of change, the ruts and rots caused by the inability to ask new or basic questions and to work intelligently toward verifiable answers.

The best illustration of this point can be found in the fact that those who *do* question must drop out of the "Establishment." The price of maintaining membership in the Establishment is unquestioning acceptance of authority.

We are, of course, aware that there are more structures than the school affecting or controlling behavior. One must be careful in identifying and discriminating among the media which have taught us how to behave. They do not teach the same thing. They do not all convey the same messages. As McLuhan would want us to see, an automobile, a Xerox machine, and an electric light bulb are all learning environments. So is our architecture, the A & P, and color TV. We are focusing on the school because it is capable of becoming the critical environment for promoting the beliefs and behaviors that are necessary to survival. We should like then to turn to a description of the type of learning environment which can best accomplish this.

III. The Inquiry Method

THE INQUIRY METHOD of teaching and learning is an attempt at redesigning the structure of the classroom. It is a new medium, and its messages are different from those usually communicated to students. Our purpose here is to begin to describe the "grammar" of the medium, for of all the "survival strategies" education has to offer, none is more potent or in greater need of explication than the "inquiry environment."

We begin by seeking help again from McLuhan. In particular, he provides three metaphors which offer a way into the problem. The first may be called the "label-libel" gambit. McLuhan refers constantly to the human tendency to dismiss an idea by the expedience of naming it. You libel by label. (Here, McLuhan connects again with Dewey, for no one stressed more than Dewey the emptiness of "verbal knowledge.") Find the right label for some process, and you know about it. If you know about it, you needn't think of it any further. "What is its name?" becomes a substitute for "How does it work?" While giving names to things, obviously, is an indispensable human activity, it can be a dangerous one, especially when you are trying to understand a complex and delicate process. McLuhan's point here is that a medium is a process, not a thing, which is an important reason why he has turned to the metaphor "massage." A massage is a process, and for health's sake, you are better advised to understand how it is working you over than to know what it is called. The inquiry method is a massage, a process, and nothing is especially revealed about its workings by trying to name it properly. And yet in educational circles, a very considerable part of the discussion about the inquiry method has centered on what is the most appropriate label to use in the discussion. In instances where someone wishes to dismiss the inquiry method, it is common to hear, "Oh, all you mean is the Socratic method." That serves as terminal punctuation. No more need be said. In better circumstances, serious people search for a "real" name: the inductive method, the discovery method, inquiry training, the hypothetical mode of teaching, inferential learning, the deductive-inductive method, the inductive-deductive method, and so on. We mean to disparage such labeling only mildly. Eventually, the profession will have to get its names straight so that intelligent discussions can go forward and useful refinements be noted. But the label is not the process, and in this case, the process needs scrutiny and description, not yet a taxonomy.

McLuhan's second useful metaphor is the "rearview-mirror" syndrome. He contends that most of us are incapable of understanding the impact of new media because we are like drivers whose gaze is fixed not on where we are going but on where we came from. It is not even a matter of seeing through the windshield but darkly. We are seeing clearly enough, but we are looking at the rearview mirror. Thus, the locomotive was first perceived as an "iron horse," the electric light as a powerful candle, and the radio as a thundering megaphone. A mistake, says McLuhan. These media were totally new experiences and did to us totally new things.

So it is with the inquiry method. It is *not* a refinement or extension or modification of older school environments. It is a different massage altogether, and, like the locomotive, light bulb, and radio, its impact will be unique and revolutionary. Yet the rearview-mirror syndrome is already at work. Most educators who have taken the trouble to think about the inquiry method are largely interested to know if it will accomplish the goals that older learning media have tried to achieve: Will students pass the Regents? Will they pass the College Boards? How will they do on "objective" tests? Will they absorb a great deal of information? Will they come up with the right answers? etc.

To a certain extent, rearview-mirror thinking can probably be valuable and is certainly understandable. If you were living 60 or 100 years ago, you might, quite reasonably, have been curious to know if light bulbs would help people to see better, or if trains would cut down the time it takes to get to Philadelphia. If there were a prophet available to answer your questions, he would have said Yes on both counts. But he also could have informed you that his answers had not told the whole story, or half of it, or even much of it: the light bulb and the locomotive, after all, changed the face of America, both inside and out. It is the same with a new medium of learning. It is entirely possible that the inquiry method will help students to produce answers their teachers crave, and remember them longer, and even utter them faster. But in anticipating this, you are imagining the most inconsequential part of the story. The inquiry method is not designed to do better what older environments try to do. It works you over in entirely different ways. It activates different senses, attitudes, and perceptions; it generates a different, bolder, and more potent kind of intelligence. Thus, it will cause teachers, and their tests, and their grading systems, and their curriculums to change. It will cause college admissions requirements to change. It will cause everything about education to change.

What we are driving at (the metaphor is not accidental) is that rearview-mirror thinking has resulted in some curious and largely ludicrous attempts to use inquiry methods as imitations of older learning environments. Some of these have been initiated by well-intentioned men who, nonetheless, are basically committed to the older forms and functions of school environments. Some have been initiated by publishers who want to satisfy the impulse for change that so many teachers feel, without requiring them to stray far from recognizable and secure controls. What they have produced is roughly on the level of using television to resuscitate vaudeville. At their worst, if we may do a bit of labeling ourselves, such efforts are best thought of as the Seductive Method of learning. The goal remains the same: to get into the student's head a series of assertions, definitions, and names as quickly as possible. (This is called "covering content.") The method turns out to be a set of questions posed by the teacher, text, or machine which is intended to lead the student to produce the right answers—answers that the teacher, text, or machine, by gum, knew all the time. This is sometimes called "programmed learning." So far, most students have been neither tricked nor intrigued by it. They recognize the old shell game when they see it, just as they recognize a lecture given on television as more of the same.

All of which brings us to our third metaphor, namely, the story line. One of McLuhan's insistent themes has been that the electric age has heightened our perception of structure by disrupting what he calls the lineality of information flow. We are not so ABCED-minded as before, not so sequential and compartmentalized. As McLuhan puts it, contemporary forms of communication require very little story line. The films of Fellini, Resnais, and Bergman are largely devoid of "plots." Abstract paintings tell no stories. One-liners and sayings on buttons replace the kind of joke that begins, "There was this farmer's daughter . . ." TV commercials are visual one-liners, their imagery being episodic, not sequential. Even newspapers, which might be thought of (to paraphrase *Peyton Place*) as the "continuing story of our culture," do not present continuous stories at all. Their stories are characterized precisely by their lack of continuity. We have small pieces of news—bits, as it were—which the reader must organize into some meaningful pattern. Monday's headline about a murder in Brooklyn disappears on Tuesday, to be replaced by one about an earthquake in Chile, which on Wednesday becomes one about an airplane crash in Beirut. Why, even *Peyton Place* itself is not in fact a "continuing story" but a fitful, almost spastic montage of emotional binges.

McLuhan contends that, without the distraction of a story line, we get a very high degree of participation and involvement in the *forms* of communication, which is another way of saying the processes of learning. One has to work hard, and one wants to, at discovering patterns and assigning meanings to one's experiences. The focus of intellectual energy becomes the active investigation of structures and relationships, rather than the passive reception of someone else's story. Of course, the school syllabus is exactly the latter: someone else's story. And most traditional learning environments are arranged to facilitate the sending and receiving of various story lines. That is why teachers regard it as desirable for students to pay attention, face front, sit up in their seats, and be quiet. "There were these Indians, see, and they lived in America before it was discovered. . . ."

The inquiry method is very much a product of our electric age. It makes the syllabus obsolete; students generate their own stories by becoming involved in the methods of learning. Where the older school environment has asked, "Who discovered America?" the inquiry method asks, "How do you discover who discovered America?" The older school environments stressed that learning is being told what happened. The inquiry environment stresses that learning is a happening in itself.

Of course, this is not the first time that such an environment has existed. Socrates had no story line to communicate and, therefore, no syllabus. His teaching was essentially *about* process; his method, his message. It is indiscreet but necessary to allude to how he ended up. His accusers cannot be faulted. They understood perfectly well the political implications of such a learning environment. *All authorities get nervous when learning is conducted without a syllabus.*

Even John Dewey was forced to concede the validity of the conservative position: once you start a man thinking, there is no telling where he will go. Just as unnerving is the fact that there is no telling *how* he will go. A syllabus not only prescribes what story lines you must learn (The War of 1812 in the sixth grade, chromosomes in the eleventh, South America in the ninth), it also prescribes the order in which your skills must be learned (spelling on Monday, grammar on Tuesday, vocabulary on Wednesday). This is called the "sequential curriculum," and one has to visit the Ford Motor plant in Detroit in order to understand fully the assumptions on which it is based. In fact, the similarities between mass-production industries and most existing school environments are striking: five-day week, seven-hour day, one hour for lunch, careful division of labor for both teachers and students, a high premium on conformity and a corresponding suspicion of originality (or any deviant behavior), and, most significantly, the administration's concern for product rather than process. But the larger point is that the sequential curriculum is inadequate because students are not sequential: most significant learning processes do not occur in linear, compartmentalized sequences. We will speak about various metaphors of the mind in a later chapter. Here, we want to say that lineal, mechanistic, input-output, ABCED-minded metaphors have been found to be increasingly unsatisfactory in our electronic age. Even professional educators, who are generally the last people to recognize the obsolescence of their own assumptions, have discovered this, and have recently invented what is called the "spiral curriculum." Unfortunately, students aren't spiral any more than they are sequential. Nonetheless, the spiral, or coil, image does have obvious advantages over its predecessor. Of course, it is still much, much too orderly to reflect what actually happens when people are engaged enthusiastically and energetically in the process of learning. Certainly, anyone who has worked with children in an inquiry environment knows what a delightful, fitful, episodic, explosive collage of simultaneous "happenings" learning is. If the learning process must be visualized, perhaps it is most authentically represented in a Jackson Pollack canvas—a canvas whose colors increase in intensity as intellectual power grows (for learning *is* exponentially cumulative).

From all of this, you must not conclude that there is no logic to the learning process. There is. But it is best described as a "psycho-logic," whose rules, sequences, spirals, and splotches are established by living, squirming, questioning, perceiving, fearing, loving, above all, languaging nervous systems. Bear in mind that the purpose of the inquiry method is to help learners increase their competence *as learners*. It hopes to accomplish this by having students *do* what effective learners do. Thus, the only reasonable kind of logic or structure that can be applied in this environment is that which is modeled after the *behavior of good learners*. Good learners, like everyone else, are living, squirming, questioning, perceiving, fearing, loving, and languaging nervous systems, but they are good learners precisely because they *believe* and *do* certain things that less effective learners do not believe and do. And therein lies the key.

What do good learners believe? What do good learners do?

First, good learners have *confidence* in their ability to learn. This does not mean that they are not sometimes frustrated and discouraged. They are, even as are poor learners. But they have a profound faith that they are capable of solving problems, and if they fail at one problem, they are not incapacitated in confronting another.

Good learners tend to *enjoy* solving problems. The process interests them, and they tend to resent people who want to "help" by giving them the answers.

Good learners seem to know what is relevant to their survival and what is not. They are apt to resent being told that something is "good for them to know," unless, of course, their crap detector advises them that it *is* good for them to know—in which case, they resent being told anyway.

Good learners, in other words, prefer to rely on their own judgment. They recognize, especially as they get older, that an incredible number of people do not know what they are talking about most of the time. As a consequence, they are suspicious of "authorities," especially any authority who discourages others from relying on their own judgment.

Good learners are usually not fearful of being wrong. They recognize their limitations and suffer no trauma in concluding that what they believe is apparently not so. In other words, they can change their minds. Changing the character of their minds is what good learners are most interested in doing.

Good learners are emphatically not fast answerers. They tend to delay their judgments until they have access to as much nformation as they imagine will be available.

Good learners are flexible. While they almost always have a point of view about a situation, they are capable of shifting to other perspectives to see what they can find. Another way of saying this is that good learners seem to understand that "answers" are relative, that everything depends on the system within which you are working. What is "true" in one system may not be "true" in another. That is why, when asked a question, good learners frequently begin their answers with the words "It depends."

Good learners have a high degree of respect for facts (which they understand are tentative) and are skillful in making distinctions between statements of fact and other kinds of statements. Good learners, for the most part, are highly skilled in all the language behaviors that comprise what we call "inquiry." For example, they know how to ask meaningful questions; they are persistent in examining their own assumptions; they use definitions and metaphors as instruments for their thinking and are rarely trapped by their own language; they are apt to be cautious and precise in making generalizations, and they engage continually in verifying what they believe; they are careful observers and seem to recognize that language tends to obscure differences and control perceptions.

Perhaps most importantly, good learners do not *need* to have an absolute, final, irrevocable resolution to every problem. The sentence, "I don't know," does not depress them, and they certainly prefer it to the various forms of semantic nonsense that pass for "answers" to questions that do not as yet have any solution—or may never have one.

If you will grant that these are some of the major beliefs and doings of good learners, then you will grasp the meaning of what we have been calling the "inquiry method." We are talking about an environment in which these behaviors can flourish, in which they are the dominant messages of the medium. Obviously, this cannot happen if you "teach" self-reliance on Monday, enjoyment of problem solving on Tuesday, and confidence on Wednesday. But neither will you get anywhere by teaching question asking in the sixth grade, observing in the seventh, and generalizing in the eighth. What we are talking about is an environment in which the full spectrum of learning behaviors—both attitudes and skills—is being employed all the time. From problem to problem. From kindergarten to graduate school. So that anytime someone is in school, he is trying to behave the way good learners behave. Only in that way can the medium convey the kinds of messages we are talking about.

Now, in practical terms, what would such an environment be made of? It seems to us that it would have four major components: the teacher, the students, the problems, and the strategies for solving problems.

Let us consider here the teachers, and especially their *attitudes*. We take it as axiomatic that the attitudes of teachers are the most important characteristic of the inquiry environment. This point is frequently passed over even by those who advocate the use of inquiry methods, but especially by those innovators who are in constant quest of "teacher-proof" programs and methodologies. *There can be no significant innovation in education that does not have at its center the attitudes of teachers, and it is an illusion to think otherwise.* The beliefs, feelings, and assumptions of teachers are the air of a learning environment; they determine the quality of life within it.

When the air is polluted, the student is poisoned, unless, of course, he holds his breath. (Not breathing is widely used by students as a defense against intellectual poison, but it mostly results, as you can imagine, in suicide by suffocation.)

The attitudes of the inquiry teacher are reflected in his behavior. When you see such a teacher in action, you observe the following:

The teacher rarely tells students what he thinks they ought to know. He believes that telling, when used as a basic teaching strategy, deprives students of the excitement of doing their own finding and of the opportunity for increasing their power as learners.

His basic mode of discourse with students is questioning. While he uses both convergent and divergent questions, he regards the latter as the more important tool. He emphatically does not view questions as a means of seducing students into parroting the text or syllabus; rather, he sees questions as instruments to open engaged minds to unsuspected possibilities.

Generally, he does not accept a single statement as an answer to a question. In fact, he has a persisting aversion to anyone, any syllabus, any text that offers The Right Answer. Not because answers and solutions are unwelcome—indeed, he is trying to help students be more efficient problem solvers —but because he knows how often The Right Answer serves only to terminate further thought. He knows the power of pluralizing. He does not ask for the reason, but for the reasons. Not for the cause, but the causes. Never the meaning, the meanings. He knows, too, the power of contingent thinking. He is the most "It depends" learner in his class.

He encourages student-student interaction as opposed to student-teacher interaction. And generally he avoids acting as a mediator or judge of the quality of ideas expressed. If each person could have with him at all times a full roster of authorities, perhaps it would not be necessary for individuals to make independent judgments. But so long as this is not possible, the individual must learn to depend on himself as a thinker. The inquiry teacher is interested in students' developing their own criteria or standards for judging the quality, precision, and relevance of ideas. He permits such development to occur by minimizing his role as arbiter of what is acceptable and what is not.

He rarely summarizes the positions taken by students on the learnings that occur. He recognizes that the act of summary or "closure" tends to have the effect of ending further thought. Because he regards learning as a process, not a terminal event, his "summaries" are apt to be stated as hypotheses, tendencies, and directions. He assumes that no one ever learns once and for all how to write, or how to read, or what were the causes of the Civil War. Rather, he assumes that one is always in the process of acquiring skills, assimilating new information, formulating or refining generalizations. Thus, he is always cautious about defining the limits of learning, about saying, "This is what you have learned during the past 45 minutes," or "This is what you will learn between now and the Christmas holidays," or even (especially), "This is what you will learn in the ninth grade." The only significant terminal behavior he recognizes is death, and he suspects that those who talk of learning as some kind of "terminal point" are either compulsive travelers or have simply not observed children closely enough. Moreover, he recognizes that learning does not occur with the same intensity in any two people, and he regards verbal attempts to disregard this fact as a semantic fiction. If a student has arrived at a particular conclusion, then little is gained by the teacher's restating it. If the student has not arrived at a conclusion, then it is presumptuous and dishonest for the teacher to contend that he has. (Any teacher who tells you precisely what his students learned during any lesson, unit, or semester quite literally does not know what he is talking about.)

His lessons develop from the responses of students and not from a previously determined "logical" structure. The only kind of lesson plan, or syllabus, that makes sense to him is one that tries to predict, account for, and deal with the authentic responses of learners to a particular problem: the kinds of questions they will ask, the obstacles they will face, their attitudes, the possible solutions they will offer, etc. Thus, he is rarely frustrated or inconvenienced by "wrong answers," false starts, irrelevant directions. These are the stuff of which his best lessons and opportunities are made. In short, the "content" of his lessons are the responses of his students. Since he is concerned with the processes of thought rather than the end results of thought (The Answer!), he does not feel compelled to "cover ground" (there's the traveler again), or to insure that his students embrace a particular doctrine, or to exclude a student's idea because it is not germane. (Not germane to what? Obviously, it is germane to the student's thinking about the problem.) He is engaged in exploring the *way* students think, not what they should think (before the Christmas holidays). That is why he spends more of his time listening to students than talking to or at them.

Generally, each of his lessons poses a problem for students. Almost all of his questions, proposed activities, and assignments are aimed at having his students clarify a problem, make observations relevant to the solution of the problem, and make generalizations based on their observations. His goal is to engage students in those activities which produce knowledge: defining, questioning, observing, classifying, generalizing, verifying, applying. As we have said, *all knowledge is a result of these activities.* Whatever we think we "know" about astronomy, sociology, chemistry, biology, linguistics, etc., was discovered or invented by someone who was more or less an expert in using inductive methods of inquiry. Thus, our inquiry, or "inductive," teacher is largely interested in helping his students to become more proficient as users of these methods.

He measures his success in terms of behavioral changes in students: the frequency with which they ask questions; the increase in the relevance and cogency of their questions; the frequency and conviction of their challenges to assertions made by other students or teachers or textbooks; the relevance and clarity of the standards on which they base their challenges; their willingness to suspend judgments when they have insufficient data; their willingness to modify or otherwise change their position when data warrant such change; the increase in their skill in observing, classifying, generalizing, etc.; the increase in their tolerance for diverse answers; their ability to apply generalizations, attitudes, and information to novel situations.

These behaviors and attitudes amount to a definition of a different *role* for the teacher from that which he has traditionally assumed. The inquiry environment, like any other school environment, is a series of human encounters, the nature of which is largely determined by the "teacher." "Teacher" is here placed in quotation marks to call attention to the fact that most of its conventional meanings are inimical to inquiry methods. It is not uncommon, for example, to hear "teachers" make statements such as, "Oh, I taught them that, but they didn't learn it." There is no utterance made in the Teachers' Room more extraordinary than this. From our point of view, it is on the same level as a salesman's remarking, "I sold it to him, but he didn't buy it"—which is to say, it makes no sense. It seems to mean that "teaching" is what a "teacher" does, which, in turn, may or may not bear any relationship to what those being "taught" do.

We are probably not being extreme when we say that about 95 percent of what is called "schooling" in America (at least above the third grade) is based on this distinction between "teaching" and "learning." Perhaps there is a need to invent a new term or name for the adult who is responsible for arranging the school learning environment. Certainly, we have discovered in our attempts to install inquiry environments in various schools that great strides can be made if the words "teach" and "teaching" are simply subtracted from the operational lexicon. When they are, a dramatic difference in behavior sometimes results. As might be expected, when the words are denied to the "teacher," there is an initial stage of extreme difficulty in talking about what will be done. There is an awkward groping for synonymous terms None come easily, especially if you also subtract "course of study," "covering ground," and several other pernicious metaphors that have the effect of subtracting the learner from your calculations. Then, almost imperceptibly, in response to questions about what one wants students to learn (as distinct from questions about what one wants to "teach" them), remarks are made in which the student, rather than the "subject," is central. Of such small language shifts, revolutions can be made. But lest you think us too romantic, we must state that we are as aware as anyone that the kind of "teacher" needed to make an inquiry environment will not be produced solely or even largely by semantic ingenuity.

Later, we will devote a chapter to some practical and bizarre suggestions, as well as bizarre practical suggestions, for inducing the condition of mind that is required of teachers in an inquiry environment. Here, we want to stress that, when the teacher assumes new functions and exhibits different behaviors, so do his students. It is in the nature of their transaction. And nothing is more important to know about inquiry methods than this.

IV. Pursuing Relevance

PICTURE THIS SCENE: Dr. Gillupsie has grouped around him several of the young resident surgeons at Blear General Hospital. They are about to begin their weekly analysis of the various operations they have performed in the preceding four days. Gillupsie nods in the direction of Jim Kildear, indicating that Kildear's cases will be discussed first:

GILLUPSIE: Well, Jim, what have you been up to this week?

KILDEAR: Only one operation. I removed the gall bladder of the patient in Room 421.

GILLUPSIE: What was his trouble?

KILDEAR: Trouble? No trouble. I believe it's just inherently good to remove gall bladders.

GILLUPSIE: Inherently good?

KILDEAR: I mean good in itself. I'm talking about removing gall bladders *qua* removing gall bladders.

GILLUPSIE: Oh; you mean removing gall bladders *per se.*

KILDEAR: Precisely, Chief. Removing his gall bladder had intrinsic merit. It was, as we say, good for its own sake.

GILLUPSIE: Splendid, Jim. If there's one thing I won't tolerate at Blear, it's a surgeon who is merely practical. What's in store next week?

KILDEAR: Two frontal lobotomies.

GILLUPSIE: Frontal lobotomies *qua* frontal lobotomies, I hope?

KILDEAR: What else?

GILLUPSIE: How about you, young Dr. Fuddy? What have you done this week?

FUDDY: Busy. Performed four pilonidal-cyst excisions.

GILLUPSIE: Didn't know we had that many cases.

FUDDY: We didn't, but you know how fond I am of pilonidal-cyst excisions. That was my major in medical school, you know.

GILLUPSIE: Of course, I'd forgotten. As I remember it now, the prospect of doing pilonidal-cyst excisions brought you into medicine, didn't it?

FUDDY: That's right, Chief. I was always interested in that. Frankly, I never cared much for appendectomies.

GILLUPSIE: Appendectomies?

FUDDY: Well, that seemed to be the trouble with the patient in 397.

GILLUPSIE: But you stayed with the old pilonidal-cyst excision, eh?

FUDDY: Right, Chief.

GILLUPSIE: Good work, Fuddy. I know just how you feel. When I was a young man, I was keenly fond of hysterectomies.

FUDDY [*giggling*]: Little tough on the men, eh, Chief?

GILLUPSIE: Well, yes [*snickering*]. But you'd be surprised at how much a resourceful surgeon can do. [*Then, solemnly.*] Well, Carstairs, how have things been going?

CARSTAIRS: I'm afraid I've had some bad luck, Dr. Gillupsie. No operations this week, but three of my patients died.

GILLUPSIE: Well, we'll have to do something about this, won't we? What did they die of?

CARSTAIRS: I'm not sure, Dr. Gillupsie, but I did give each one of them plenty of penicillin.

GILLUPSIE: Ah! The traditional "good for its own sake" approach, eh, Carstairs?

CARSTAIRS: Well, not exactly, Chief. I just thought that penicillin would help them get better.

GILLUPSIE: What were you treating them for?

CARSTAIRS: Well, each one was awful sick, Chief, and I know that penicillin helps sick people get better.

GILLUPSIE: It certainly does, Carstairs. I think you acted wisely.

CARSTAIRS: And the deaths, Chief?

GILLUPSIE: Bad patients, son, bad patients. There's nothing a good doctor can do about bad patients. And there's nothing a good medicine can do for bad patients, either.

CARSTAIRS: But still, I have a nagging feeling that perhaps they didn't *need* penicillin, that they might have needed something else.

GILLUPSIE: Nonsense! Penicillin never fails to work on good patients. We all know that. I wouldn't worry too much about it, Carstairs.

Perhaps our playlet needs no further elaboration, but we want to underscore some of its points. First, had we continued the conversation between Dr. Gillupsie and his young surgeons, we could easily have included a half dozen other "reasons" for inflicting upon children the kinds of irrelevant curricula that comprise most of conventional schooling. For example, we could have had one doctor still practicing "bleeding" his patients because he had not yet discovered that such practices do no good. Another doctor could have insisted that he has "cured" his patients in spite of the fact that they have all died. ("Oh, I taught them that, but they didn't learn it.") Still another doctor might have defended some practice by reasoning that, although his operation didn't do much for the patient now, in later life the patient might have need for exactly this operation, and if he did, *voilà!*, it will already have been done.

The second point we would like to make is that we have not "made up" these "reasons." Our playlet is a parody only in the sense that it is inconceivable for doctors to have such conversations. Had we, instead, used a principal and his teachers, and if they discussed what was "taught" during the week, and why, our playlet would have been a documentary, and not a heavy-handed one, either. There are thousands of teachers who believe that there are certain subjects that are "inherently good," that are "good in themselves," that are "good for their own sake." When you ask "Good for whom?" or "Good for what purpose?" you will be dismissed as being "merely practical" and told that what they are talking about is literature *qua* literature, grammar *qua* grammar, and mathematics *per se*. Such people are commonly called "humanists."

There are thousands of teachers who teach "subjects" such as Shakespeare, or the Industrial Revolution, or geometry because *they* are inclined to enjoy talking about such matters. In fact, that is why they became teachers. It is also why their students fail to become competent learners. There are thousands of teachers who define a "bad" student as any student who doesn't respond to what has been prescribed for him. There are still thousands more who teach one thing or another under the supposition that the "subject" will do something for their students which, in fact, it does not do, and never did, and, indeed, which most evidence indicates, does just the opposite. And so on.

The third point we would like to make about our analogy is that the "trouble" with all these "reasons" is that they leave out the (patient) learner, which is really another way of saying that they leave out reality. With full awareness of the limitations of our patient-learner metaphor, we would assert that it is insane (literally or metaphorically, take your pick) to perform a pilonidal-cyst excision unless your patient requires it to maintain his comfort and health; *and* it is also insane (again, take your pick as to how) for a teacher to "teach" something unless his students require it for some identifiable and important purpose, which is to say, for some purpose that is related to the life of the learner. *The survival of the learner's skill and interest in learning is at stake.* And we feel that, in saying this, we are not being melodramatic.

Recently, we attended a state convention of supervisors of teachers of English. The state in question has had a troubled and ugly history of racial crisis. Its people are struggling, against themselves, to adopt attitudes America desperately needs. Like other states, this one has had many of its young men in Vietnam, killing and being killed for reasons not all Americans support. Poverty is no stranger to this state. Nor is censorship, The John Birch Society, or a dozen other issues and quarrels that separate Americans from each other and from a satisfactory meeting with the future. Since all of these problems are human problems, in one way or another they are touched, shaped, even created by language. Could there be, then, a more interesting meeting to attend than one convened by supervisors of teachers concerned primarily with language and its uses? Early in the proceedings a man rose to ask a question about linguistics, for that was the main topic of the conference. "What we want to know," he asked the assembled experts, "is which grammar should we teach?" Now, what would you suppose to be the response of an audience of mature, responsible educators to such a question? Laughter perhaps, at a feeble attempt at irony? Annoyance maybe, for the time it wastes? Disgust, in a measure equal to the seriousness of the questioner? Wrong. There was applause. Warm, fully approving applause. The man was right. That was exactly what the audience wanted to know, and the answer it received was also warmly appreciated: teach all of the grammars, and prepare yourself to teach, as well, those yet to come.

Where is the learner in all of this? Where is his world? Let's try again. Below is the complete review of a new (1967) series of English texts (grades one through eight). The review was written by an assistant editor of an important educational journal (we did *not* "make it up"):

> At first glance the busy school administrator is likely to think, "Oh, no! Not another language series! If you've seen one, you've seen them all."
>
> However, a careful examination of these brand-new books reveals features which haven't been seen in other series and which are most commendable.
>
> The first thing to catch the eye, and quite properly so, is

the title "English" on every book. For many years elementary-textbook authors and publishers have called this subject "Language" when taught in the grade school—as though they were assiduously avoiding any title which might sound like the name of a difficult high-school or college course.

And English it is! In an introductory supplement the authors define three types of grammar (in the old days there were only two: good and bad) and go on to say their "eclectic approach" makes use of all of them.

It does seem that the books have unashamedly made use of the vocabulary of traditional grammar without detracting from their appeal to pupils with elementary-school vocabularies. The emphasis, of course, is on function rather than terminology.

It is this emphasis on good usage from the first grade up which should endear the series to teachers who are themselves users of good English. Whether the grammar is called traditional, structural, or transformational matters very little.

Throughout the entire elementary-grade series there is a consistent chapter structure. Each chapter is introduced by a full-page illustration plus a "Do You Know?" list of items indicating the content of that chapter. Then follows an opening block of linguistic lessons, a group of lessons called "Working with Words," an instructional unit on "Using Linguistics," and a concluding series designed to provide review, check-up, self-evaluation, and additional practice.

The fact that all chapters in all books follow this pattern gives assurance that the series has been carefully planned. The authors seem to have achieved this consistency with very little resultant monotony.

Somewhere in the middle of every chapter is a poem or group of poems for study and discussion.

Except for the consumable first-grade edition, all of the books are hard-bound in colorful board covers and are well-illustrated with "integrated" illustrations. The pictures show children of different races and nationalities together in various social situations.

In the teachers' edition of the junior-high-school volumes there are two parts of the blue-page introductory section which could well be required reading for all English teachers: Part 2 on "Basic Concepts of Language Instruction" and Part 3 on

"English in the Total Curriculum." This philosophy is sound regardless of the basic textbook being used.

Now, it strikes us that this is a most curious statement, all the more so because it is in no sense untypical. Even if one disregards the fatuousness of the writing (how could anyone who writes like this evaluate an English book?), there are probably dozens of questions that someone who is acquainted with reality would want to ask of the reviewer, among which would be to wonder why he is so taken by the fact that the books have the word "English" on the cover rather than "Language." But from our point of view, the most striking feature of the review is that it makes only *one* mention of the learners whom the texts are supposed to affect. That reference is in itself extraordinary: "It does seem that the books have unashamedly made use of the vocabulary of traditional grammar without detracting from their *appeal to pupils* with elementary-school vocabularies." (Our italics.) Appeal to pupils? Whose pupils are these? From what world do they come? Could there be pupils anywhere who would find *appeal* in anything described in this review? Such as, for example, that the books use an eclectic approach to grammar? Or that they have the word "English" on the cover? Or that the books emphasize "good English"? (*There's* a novelty for you!) Or perhaps that the books have a consistent chapter structure ("with very little resultant monotony") and abundant opportunities for review, check-up, self-evaluation, and additional practice?

We will avoid the temptation of writing another playlet in which fourth-graders Irving and Charlie discuss the appeal that their new series of English texts holds for them. It would probably be unfair. Besides, there is something far more dramatic for us to present on the subject of relevance in education. It does not come from an educational journal. Nor was it written by professional educators. It is, of course, "subversive." It is an excerpt from *Let Us Now Praise Famous Men* by James Agee and Walker Evans. In 1936, Agee and Evans lived with a family of Alabama farmers in order to prepare themselves to produce a document on cotton tenantry in the United States. As Evans took his remarkable photographs of these people and their environment, Agee studied the various institutions that impinged on their lives. One of them was school. Here is Agee on the curriculum in Alabama in 1936:

> Or again on the curriculum: it was unnecessary to make even such search into this as I made to know that there is no setting before the students of "economic" or "social" or "political" "facts" and of their situation within these "facts," no attempt made to clarify or even slightly to relieve the situation between the white and Negro races, far less to explain the sources, no attempt to clarify psychological situations in the individual, in his family, or in his world, no attempt to get beneath and to revise those "ethical" and "social" pressures and beliefs in which even a young child is trapped, no attempt, beyond the most nominal, to interest a child in using or in discovering his senses and judgment, no attempt to counteract the paralytic quality inherent in "authority," no attempt beyond the most nominal and stifling to awaken, to protect, or to "guide" the sense of investigation, the sense of joy, the sense of beauty, no attempt to clarify spoken and written words whose power of deceit even at the simplest is vertiginous, no attempt, or very little, and ill taught, to teach even the earliest techniques of improvement in occupation ("scientific farming," diet and cooking, skilled trades), nor to "teach" a child in terms of his environment, no attempt, beyond the most suffocated, to awaken a student either to "religion" or "irreligion," no attempt to develop in him either "skepticism" or "faith," nor "wonder," nor mental "honesty" nor mental "courage," nor any understanding of or delicateness in "the emotions" and in any of the uses and pleasures of the body save the athletic; no attempt either to relieve him of fear and of poison in sex or to release in him a free beginning of pleasure in it, nor to open within him the illimitable potentials of grief, of danger, and of goodness in sex and in sexual love, nor to give him the beginnings at very least of a knowledge, and of an attitude, whereby he may hope to guard and increase himself and those whom he touches, no indication of the damages which society, money, law, fear and quick belief have set

upon these matters and upon all things in human life, nor of their causes, nor of the alternate ignorances and possibilities of ruin or of joy, no fear of doubtlessness, no fear of the illusions of knowledge, no fear of compromise.

There are several things we want to say about this stunning piece of prose; the first, that it *is* stunning, and that we understand thoroughly your impulse to abandon the book before you and seek out *Let Us Now Praise Famous Men*. The second is that, with few exceptions (for example, an increased attention to vocational training), Agee's condemnation of the school curriculum circa 1936 *is entirely applicable to the present day*. In plain truth, what passes for a curriculum in today's schools is little else but a strategy of distraction, as it was in Alabama in 1936. It is largely designed to *keep* students from knowing themselves and their environment in any realistic sense; which is to say, it does not allow inquiry into most of the critical problems that comprise the content of the world outside the school. (In this connection—we will say more of it later—one of the main differences between the "advantaged" student and the "disadvantaged" is that the former has an *economic* stake in giving his attention to the curriculum while the latter does not. In other words, the only relevance of the curriculum for the "advantaged" student is that, if he does what he is told, there will be a tangible payoff.)

Below is a piece of the curriculum of a modern school. It is a "good" school, which means, to the people who call it "good," that there are few Negroes in it, that the parents of many of the children want them to go to college, that the school is housed in an expensive physical setting, that there are few serious "reading" problems, and that the students get high scores (one way or another) on state-wide or national tests:

> We owe a great debt to the ancient civilization of Egypt, Greece, and Rome especially in art, literature, science and government. Since this is such an important unit we will study *each* country separately beginning with Egypt; then we will study Greece and lastly Rome. For each of these peoples there

will be a list of questions and a list of projects. You will each write the answers to *all* of the questions. Everyone will do one project for each country being studied. These may be done alone or in a small group of no more than three members.

The following books will help you to get started. Read at least two of those suggested before you begin to answer the questions or to work on your projects. You are expected to obtain at least two (2) other books from the library and to read no less than thirty (30) pages about each country. . . .

QUESTIONS

Ancient Egypt

1. How were the Egyptians affected by the climate and geography of their country? Discuss the following in your answer:
   a. an oasis
   b. living in a desert area
   c. irrigation
   d. delta
   e. safety from warring tribes

2. What were some of the ways of earning a living in ancient Egypt? Include the following in your answer:
   a. agriculture
   b. manufacturing
   c. education
   d. government jobs
   e. any others you find in your reading. . . .

Ancient Greece

1. Who were the ancient Greeks? Where did they come from? How did the geography of Greece affect them?

2. Why was Athens the leading city in Greece? What is a city-state?

3. How many languages were spoken in Greece? How did this affect Greek life?

4. What sort of religion did the ancient Greeks have? How does this compare to that of the Egyptians?

The most depressing aspect of this piece of pretentious trivia is that to most people nothing seems wrong with it. Indeed, it may even be thought of as reflecting a "progressive" idea or two. (After all, aren't the students asked to work in small groups and do "projects"?) Clearly, defenders of "high standards" would have no cause for complaint here. The same is true for makers of standardized texts, "transmitters of our cultural heritage," and lovers of "basic education" everywhere. Perhaps even most of the students for whom this "unit of work" is intended would approve of it. But if they do, we can be sure their approval rests largely on a carefully cultivated schizophrenia that is necessary, in present circumstances, to their academic survival. (Mencken once wrote that the main thing children learn in school is how to lie.) The children *know* that none of these questions has anything to do with them, and the game that is being played does not require that the questions do. The game is called "Let's Pretend," and if its name were chiseled into the front of every school building in America, we would at least have an honest announcement of what takes place there. The game is based on a series of pretenses which include: Let's pretend that you are not what you are and that this sort of work makes a difference to your lives; let's pretend that what bores you is important, and that the more you are bored, the more important it is; let's pretend that there are certain things *everyone* must know, and that both the questions and answers about them have been fixed for all time; let's pretend that your intellectual competence can be judged on the basis of how well you can play Let's Pretend.

Of course, what you have here is a classic "put on." But an extremely dangerous one because the participants are not fully conscious of the sham. Its most devastating effect is to produce in students a feeling of alienation from the educational process. G. B. Shaw's line that the only time his education was interrupted was when he was in school captures the sense of this alienation. The learner comes to understand that what he is asked to think about in school has no bearing on what he needs to learn to think about. He, therefore, removes the best, the most vital part of himself from his formal education. He realizes, too, that the standards used to judge his school performance lack authenticity, and his contempt for such standards is widespread and (from the perspective of his teachers) scandalous. Consider the *meaning* of the following article from *The New York Post*, Wednesday, April 26, 1967:

THE CHEATING SCANDAL:
FOUR BOYS ON THE CARPET

by Leonard Katz

Authorities at DeWitt Clinton HS in the Bronx today were studying what punishment to hand out to four seniors who distributed stolen copies of midterm exams.

And some 2,000 Clinton students were stewing over the news that they must take the tests over.

Principal Walter J. Degnan yesterday ordered all English, economics, and American history tests taken over after learning that the tests had been stolen and the answers passed around the school in one of the city's worst public-school cheating incidents.

The seniors who took the tests had "impeccable" records, authorities said. But they used master keys to take the tests from storerooms before they were given.

The keys were given them by a supervisor for whom they worked in the school's night community center at Mosholu Pkwy. and Paul Avenue.

Boys Bragged

The answer sheets were spread around and the boys began "to brag a little and word filtered back," a Board of Education spokesman said.

But not before the tests—which won't be graded now—were given.

All but one student in an informal poll denied benefiting from the answers but most believed they would suffer on the second test.

"It's a bomb," said Raymond Rodriguez Jr., 17, a junior of 960 Simpson St. "It's not fair. I didn't know anything about it, but I know I passed. Why should I put myself on the line again?"

Edward Torres, 18, of 1997 Vyse Ave., agreed. "Lots of kids will do worse the second time around," he said. "Not because they cheated or anything, but you study for the big day and then you take the test and then you forget what you studied."

Felix Figueroa, 17, a junior of 585 Union Ave., said, "It's unfair to everybody. The ones caught cheating are the ones who should be made to take the test over. Not the whole school."

But Domingo Maldonado, 17, a junior of 936 E. 172 St. said re-testing was fair "as far as I'm concerned. They can't ask you anything you haven't covered in class. I'll probably do better the second time.

"At least now I'll have an idea of what the test will be like."

A senior, who withheld his name, admitted he had received the answers to the English test.

"Man," he said, "I'll never pass. I've been flunking this . . . subject all term and I'll never pass without the answers."

Beautiful, isn't it? The students all had "impeccable" records but Rodriguez doesn't want to put himself on the line again, and Torres knows how easily you forget what you studied, and Figueroa is teed-off at the ones who were *caught* cheating, and Maldonado figures he'll finally know in advance what a test is going to be like, and an unnamed senior is worried because, without the answers, he knows he's finished. What kind of vicious game is being played here, and who are the sinners and who the sinned against?

This state of affairs—these chilling remarks by totally alienated students—is a result of a severe ecological imbalance. Ecology has to do with the relationship of all the elements of an environment, and how these relationships lead to balance and survival, and how they lead to imbalance and death. In the learning environment, there are at least four critical elements: the learner, the teacher, the "to-be-learned," and the strategies for learning. For this environment to fulfill its function, these elements must serve, complement, and derive meaning from each other. It simply will not do to invite students to be aggressive, independent inquirers and then insist that their inquiries focus on the ways of earning a living in Ancient Egypt. Nor will it do to put a sensitive, nonauthoritarian teacher in a classroom whose students are required, by curriculum mandate, to read at least two (2) books before they undertake their project, and to read two (2) during, and certainly not less than thirty (30) pages from each book.

There is no way to help a learner to be disciplined, active, and thoroughly engaged unless *he* perceives a problem to be a problem or whatever is to-be-learned as worth learning, and unless he plays an active role in determining the process of solution. That is the plain, unvarnished truth, and if it sounds like warmed-over "progressive education," it is not any less true for it. Moreover, if it is a truth that is susceptible of easy parody ("Well, children, what shall we study today?" "Gee, teacher, can't *you* tell us what we want to study for a change?"), so are most important truths, and so what? Besides, it really isn't much of a parody anyway since a teacher can, without injuring the learning process, suggest all sorts of things for study. No one has ever said that children themselves are the only, or necessarily the best, source for articulating relevant areas of inquiry. What *has* been said is that, regardless of its source, unless an inquiry is perceived as relevant by the learner, no significant learning will take place. No one will learn anything he doesn't want to know. And if he is made to—that is, forced to act as if he does—he and his teacher will regret it, for he then talks about learning the way Rodriguez and Torres and Maldonado do. We didn't make that up. That's the way it is.

It is sterile and ridiculous to attempt to release the inquiry powers of students by initiating studies that hold no interest for them. Have you ever seen such a performance? For example, the use of the inquiry method to discover the characteristics of pendulums or the forms of verbs? It is a kind of intellectual minuet—all form and no substance. The students behave oddly, as if they are expecting something to happen, but nothing does. Their generalizations turn out to bear no relationship to anything they care about. Reason, Plato insisted, must have an adequate emotional base if education is to accomplish its purpose. If there is no emotional base, or if it is an ersatz one, very little of significance can happen to a learner, except in the most negative terms.

For all the attention Jerome Bruner has attracted to the structure of inquiry, we probably need to hold him accountable for what might be called the "discovering your pendulum" application of the inquiry method. Bruner has done much to answer the question "How do people come to know?," but, curiously, he has not addressed himself to the question "What's worth knowing?," at least from the point of view of the learner. It is almost impossible to find in Bruner's explications of inquiry learning one illustration of children's solving problems that are of deep concern to children, although most of the problems seem to interest Bruner. Perhaps it is too much to expect of a psychologist developing a theory of instruction that he also develop a theory of *relevance* in instruction. In any case, it is not our intention to defame Jerome Bruner. Anyone advancing notions of a new education owes him much and is a scoundrel for belaboring his omissions. But the fact is that many of the innovators and experimenters who have learned from Bruner, have also learned his mistakes. They haven't much asked themselves, "What's worth knowing?" either. Thus, they have insured that there will be an ecological imbalance in the new learning environments they have tried to create.

Of all the matters of concern to children one can imagine— for example, those delineated by James Agee—very few have ever been touched by traditional learning environments. That much everybody knows. But very few have so far been touched by inquiry environments, either. We have in mind "the new math," "the new science," "the new social studies," and especially "the new English." These curricula are ostensibly devoted to the new forms of learning, such as those which we described in the last chapter, but, for the most part, these forms, or processes, have not been applied to relevant problems in the society, as those problems are perceived by learners.

Why this is so is worth talking about, we believe, for several reasons. The first, as always in matters of educational innovation, has to do with teachers. Let us take English teachers as an example and imagine that they have accepted (as in many cases they have) the idea of an essentially inquiry environment. That means creating an environment that gives the highest possible priority to inquiry behavior. It is an environment that values above all else the development of such survival attitudes and perspectives as objectivity, tentativeness, self-sufficiency, contingency, open-endedness, flexibility, inventiveness, and resourcefulness. The teachers intend to cultivate such behavior by having their students engage in question asking, defining, observing, classifying, generalizing, verifying, and all the other skills of inquiry. Thus, the "content" of the environment would seem to be a process. The medium is the message and all that. So far so good. But there is, in another sense, a "content" that has to be accounted for. What will the students think about? What are the problems they will use their inquiry skills on? Toward what matters will they apply the attitudes of competent learners?

Now, if the "subject" is what is called "English," the list of possible relevant problems is literally endless. For example, if one accepts the rather obvious fact that language is almost always produced by human beings for human purposes to share human meanings (the one exception to this is when two grammarians have a conversation), then the study of language is inseparable from the study of human situations. A language situation (i.e., a human situation) is any human event in which language is used to share meanings. A poem is a language situation. So is a joke, an expression of condolence, an editorial, an advertisement, an argument, a TV newscast, a scientific report, a song, a menu. In a later chapter, we will provide some specific questions about these and other language situations that children are extremely interested in asking. So interested, in fact, that they cannot be *stopped* from making imaginative, rigorous, and sustained inquiries into them. Here, it is merely necessary to say that each of these language situations is different from the others; that is, it has its own rules. Each is a situation about which children know a great deal, but not nearly enough. And each is a situation which is real, may easily be encountered, and is therefore useful to know about. In other words, in studying about how language works, one has available all the possible forms of human discourse to examine. So what do you think the focus of the "new English" is? *Grammar*. So help us.

Of course, we earlier alluded to this fact. But the question is, why is this so? Why have English teachers looked to grammarians for their opportunities? Why, of all the relevant and even critical language problems under the sun, have English teachers selected grammatical ones as the terrain for their students' inquiries? In answering, one must try hard not to be libelous. But the fact is that many teachers of English are fearful of life and, incidentally, of children. They are pompous and precious, and are lovers of symmetry, categories, and proper labels. For them, the language of real human activity is too sloppy, emotional, uncertain, dangerous, and thus altogether too unsettling to study in the classroom. It was Kafka, we believe, who remarked that he could not understand why some people were so disdainful of "everyday" life since that was the only one they had. He must have had in mind the kind of English teacher we are describing.

Grammarians offer such teachers a respectable out. They give them a game to play, with rules and charts, and with boxes and arrows to draw. Grammar is not, of course, without its controversies, but they are of such a sterile and generally pointless nature that only one who is widely removed from relevant human concerns can derive much stimulation from them. Browning's line that grammarians are dead from the waist down captures the sense of what we are trying to say about them. (An emphatic exception to Browning's observation is Professor Noam Chomsky, who has recently distinguished himself as an invaluable "crap detector" of the language of political bureaucrats and "house intellectuals.") We want to make it clear that we do not object to the work of grammarians, or grammarians themselves.

What we are complaining about is the incredible fact that the exotic interests of these men have been put at the center of the "new English," by teachers who are afraid to go where the feelings, perceptions, and questions of children would take them. You see, there simply aren't any children who would have any possible reason—now or for the rest of their lives—to care about how a noun is defined, or what the transformational rules are for forming the passive voice, or how many allomorphs there are of the plural morpheme. And as long as we have English teachers who think there are, the "new English," in its effects, will be virtually indistinguishable from the "old English."

The same is true of other "subjects" as well. It is close to futile to talk of any new curriculum unless you are talking about the possibility of getting a new kind of teacher—whether his "subject" is English, science, social studies, or whatever.

But it would not be wholly accurate to blame the pursuit of irrelevance entirely on teachers. We are, after all, talking about educational innovation that would produce a different kind of person from those who are valued in schools today. Many people other than teachers have a stake in such a possibility. We have in mind political and religious leaders. Bureaucrats and the bureaucratic-minded. Businessmen and advertisers, and many others, including all those who have large spiritual and material investments in the kind of mentality our schools currently produce. Consider this: The first hole ever dug on the moon by a man-made machine is now done. It is the most expensive hole in the history of the human race. Now, what does that mean? How do we know whether this is one of man's noblest achievements or if it is a game being played by a small group of lunatics for their own amusement—at our expense?

As we write, a large group of native Americans are in open rebellion against their government. There is insurrection throughout the land, as there has been before, in 1776 and 1861. How do we know if this is one of man's deepest needs expressing itself ("the language of the unheard," Dr. King called it) or if it is a mindless aberration precipitated by summer heat and boredom?

As we write, there is war in Vietnam. Fifteen thousand Americans are dead and B-52s have dropped more bombs on Vietnam than were dropped on Germany in World War II. Is this done truly in the cause of freedom—ours or someone else's—or is it a mindless madness that is self-propelling?

We do not think it unreasonable to suggest that there are many influential people who would resent such questions' being asked—in fact, would go to considerable trouble to prevent their being asked. Such people depend heavily on the continuing irrelevance of most school curricula. But this is not to say that they oppose educational innovation. On the contrary. They usually can be relied upon to give unflagging support to instructional television, team teaching, green chalk boards, movable chairs, more textbooks, teaching machines, the use of overhead projectors, and other innovations that play no role in effecting significant learning. Operating in these matters is a kind of variation of Parkinson's Law of Triviality: The enthusiasm that community leaders display for an educational innovation is in inverse proportion to its significance to the learning process.

There are, of course, still other reasons for the absence of relevance in school environments, one of which is the reluctantly acknowledged probability that our society, in general, does not much care for youth. This means that, in spite of the fact that we make available to our youth incredible sums of money, we exploit them, mock their attempts at self-expression, and do not provide them with opportunities for living "manly," dignified, and productive *adolescent* lives. The evidence for this has been put before us by, among others, Paul Goodman in *Growing Up Absurd*, Jules Henry in *Culture Against Man*, John Holt in *How Children Fail*, Edgar Friedenberg in *The Vanishing Adolescent*, and Earl Kelley in *In De-*

fense of Youth. But like other educationists, we will ignore what they have said, although for different reasons. In our case, the truth is simply too depressing, even overwhelming to face. Its acknowledgment could well drive anyone proposing educational innovation into a state of intellectual catatonia. One must make certain assumptions in order to get on with one's work. Therefore, let us assume that America values its youth, that our community leaders want our youth to know reality and not just fantasy, and that our teachers do not fear youth and their need to know about the world they live in. In that case, what's worth knowing?

V. What's Worth Knowing?

SUPPOSE all of the syllabi and curricula and textbooks in the schools disappeared. Suppose all of the standardized tests—city-wide, state-wide, and national—were lost. In other words, suppose that the most common material impeding innovation in the schools simply did not exist. Then suppose that you decided to turn this "catastrophe" into an opportunity to increase the relevance of the schools. What would you do?

We have a possibility for you to consider: suppose that you decide to have the entire "curriculum" consist of questions. These questions would have to be worth seeking answers to not only from your point of view but, more importantly, from the point of view of the students. In order to get still closer to reality, add the requirement that the questions must help the students to develop and internalize concepts that will help them to survive in the rapidly changing world of the present and future.

Obviously, we are asking you to suppose you were an educator living in the second half of the twentieth century. What questions would you have on your list?

Take a pencil and list your questions on the next page, which we have left blank for you. Please do not be concerned about defacing our book, unless, of course, one of your questions is going to be "What were some of the ways of earning a living in Ancient Egypt?" In that case, use your *own* paper.

Now, if one of your questions was something like "Why should you answer someone else's questions?," then you undoubtedly realize that we will submit our own sample list with some misgivings. As we have said, the ecology of the inquiry environment requires that the *students* play a central, but not necessarily exclusive, role in framing questions that they deem important. Even the most sensitive teacher cannot always project himself into the perspective of his students, and he dare not assume that *his* perception of reality is necessarily shared by them. With this limitation in mind, we can justify the list we will submit on several grounds. First, many of these questions *have* literally been asked by children and adolescents when they were permitted to respond freely to the challenge of "What's Worth Knowing?" Second, some of these questions are based on our careful *listening* to students, even though they were not at the time asking questions. Very often children make declarative statements about things when they really mean only to elicit an informative response. In some cases, they do this because they have learned from adults that it is "better" to pretend that you know than to admit that you don't. (An old aphorism describing this process goes: Children enter school as question marks and leave as periods.) In other cases, they do this because they do not know *how* to ask certain kinds of questions. In any event, a simple translation of their declarative utterances will sometimes produce a great variety of deeply felt questions.

Our final justification rests with our own imagination. We have framed—as we asked you to do—some questions which, in our judgment, are responsive to the actual and immediate as against the fancied and future needs of learners in the world as it *is* (not as it *was*). In this, we have not surveyed thousands of students, but have consulted with many, mostly

in junior and senior high school. We have tried variations of these questions with children in primary grades. By and large, the response was enthusiastic—and serious. There seemed to be little doubt that, from the point of view of the students, these questions made much more sense than the ones they usually have to memorize the right answers to in school. At this point it might be worth noting that our list of questions is intended to "educate" students. Contrary to conventional school practice, what that means is that we want to elicit from students the meanings that they have already stored up so that they may subject those meanings to a testing and verifying, reordering and reclassifying, modifying and extending process. In this process, the student is not a passive "recipient"; he becomes an active *producer* of knowledge. The word "educate" is closely related to the word "educe." In the oldest pedagogic sense of the term, this meant drawing out of a person something potential or latent. We can, after all, learn only in relation to what we already know. Again, contrary to common misconceptions, this means that, if we don't know very much, our capability for learning is not very great. This idea—virtually by itself—requires a major revision in most of the metaphors that shape school policies and procedures.

Reflect on these questions—and others that these can generate. Please do not merely react to them.

What do you worry about most?

What are the causes of your worries?

Can any of your worries be eliminated? How?

Which of them might you deal with first? How do you decide?

Are there other people with the same problems? How do you know? How can you find out?

If you had an important idea that you wanted to let everyone (in the world) know about, how might you go about letting them know?

What bothers you most about adults? Why?

How do you want to be similar to or different from adults you know when you become an adult?

What, if anything, seems to you to be worth dying for?

How did you come to believe this?

What seems worth living for?

How did you come to believe this?

At the present moment, what would you most like to be—or be able to do? Why? What would you have to know in order to be able to do it? What would you have to do in order to get to know it?

How can you tell "good guys" from "bad guys"?

How can "good" be distinguished from "evil"?

What kind of a person would you most like to be? How might you get to be this kind of person?

At the present moment, what would you most like to be doing? Five years from now? Ten years from now? Why? What might you have to do to realize these hopes? What might you have to give up in order to do some or all of these things?

When you hear or read or observe something, how do you know what it means?

Where does meaning "come from"?

What does "meaning" mean?

How can you tell what something "is" or whether it is?

Where do words come from?

Where do symbols come from?

Why do symbols change?

Where does knowledge come from?

What do you think are some of man's most important ideas? Where did they come from? Why? How? Now what?

What's a "good idea"?

How do you know when a good or live idea becomes a bad or dead idea?

Which of man's ideas would we be better off forgetting? How do you decide?

What is "progress"?

What is "change"?

What are the most obvious causes of change? What are the least apparent? What conditions are necessary in order for change to occur?

What kinds of changes are going on right now? Which are important? How are they similar to or different from other changes that have occurred?

What are the relationships between new ideas and change? Where do *new* ideas come from? How come? So what?

If you wanted to stop one of the changes going on now (pick one), how would you go about it? What consequences would you have to consider?

Of the important changes going on in our society, which should be encouraged and which resisted? Why? How?

What are the most important changes that have occurred in the past ten years? twenty years? fifty years? In the last year? In the last six months? Last month? What will be the most important changes next month? Next year? Next decade? How can you tell? So what?

What would you change if you could? How might you go about it? Of those changes which are going to occur, which would you stop if you could? Why? How? So what?

Who do you think has the most important things to say today? To whom? How? Why?

What are the dumbest and most dangerous ideas that are "popular" today? Why do you think so? Where did these ideas come from?

What are the conditions necessary for life to survive? Plants? Animals? Humans?

Which of these conditions are necessary for all life?

Which ones for plants? Which ones for animals? Which ones for humans?

What are the greatest threats to all forms of life? To plants? To animals? To humans?

What are some of the "strategies" living things use to survive? Which unique to plants? Which unique to animals? Which unique to humans?

What kinds of human survival strategies are (1) similar to those of animals and plants; (2) different from animals and plants?

What does man's language permit him to develop as survival strategies that animals cannot develop?

How might man's survival activities be different from what they are if he did not have language?

What other "languages" does man have besides those consisting of words?

What functions do these "languages" serve? Why and how do they originate? Can you invent a new one? How might you start?

What would happen, what difference would it make, what would man *not* be able to do if he had no number (mathematical) languages?

How many symbol systems does man have? How come? So what?

What are some good symbols? Some bad?

What good symbols could we use that we do not have?

What bad symbols do we have that we'd be better off without?

What's worth knowing? How do you decide? What are some ways to go about getting to know what's worth knowing?

It is necessary for us to say at once that these questions are not intended to represent a catechism for the new education. These are samples and illustrations of the kinds of questions we think worth answering. Our set of questions is best regarded as a metaphor of our sense of relevance. If you took the trouble to list your own questions, it is quite possible that you prefer many of them to ours. Good enough. The new education is a process and will not suffer from the applied imaginations of all who wish to be a part of it. But in evaluating your own questions, as well as ours, bear in mind that there are certain *standards* that must be used. These standards may also be stated in the form of questions:

Will your questions increase the learner's *will* as well as his capacity to learn?

Will they help to give him a sense of joy in learning?

Will they help to provide the learner with confidence in his ability to learn?

In order to get answers, will the learner be required to make inquiries? (Ask further questions, clarify terms, make observations, classify data, etc.?)

Does each question allow for alternative answers (which implies alternative modes of inquiry)?

Will the process of answering the questions tend to stress the uniqueness of the learner?

Would the questions produce different answers if asked at different stages of the learner's development?

Will the answers help the learner to sense and understand the universals in the human condition and so enhance his ability to draw closer to other people?

If the answers to these questions about your list of questions are all "yes," then you are to be congratulated for insisting upon extremely high standards in education. If that seems an unusual compliment, it is only because we have all become accustomed to a conception and a hierarchy of standards that, in our opinion, is simultaneously upside-down and irrelevant. We usually think of a curriculum as having high standards if "it" covers ground, requires much and difficult reading, demands many papers, and if the students for whom it is intended do not easily get "good" grades. Advocates of "high standards" characteristically and unwittingly invoke other revealing metaphors. One of the most frequently used of these is "basic fundamentals." The most strident advocates of "high, and ever yet higher, standards" insist that these be "applied" particularly to "basic fundamentals." Indulging our propensity to inquire into the language of education, we find that the essential portion of the word "fundamental" is the word "fundament." It strikes us as poetically appropriate that "fundament" also means the buttocks, and specifically the anus. We will resist the temptation to explore the unconscious motives of "fundamentalists." But we cannot resist saying that *their* "high standards" represent the *lowest possible standards imaginable* in any conception of a new education. In fact, so low, that the up-down metaphor is not very useful in describing it.

What one needs to ask of a standard is not, "Is it high or low?," but, "Is it appropriate to your goals?" If your goals are to make people more alike, to prepare them to be be docile functionaries in some bureaucracy, and to prevent them from being vigorous, self-directed learners, then the standards of most schools are neither high nor low. They are simply apt. If the goals are those of a new education, one needs standards based on the actual activities of competent, confident learners when they are genuinely engaged in learning. One must be centrally concerned with the hearts and minds of learners—in contrast to those merely concerned with the "fundament." No competent learner ever says to himself, "In trying to solve this problem, I will read two books (not less than 30 pages from each). Then, I will make a report of not less than 20 pages, with a minimum of 15 footnotes. . . ." The only place one finds such "standards" is in a school syllabus. *They do not exist in natural, human learning situations, since they have nothing to do with the conditions of learning—with what the learner needs to be and to do in order to learn about learning, or indeed about anything.* Any talk about high standards from teachers or school administrators is nonsense unless they are talking about *standards of learning* (as distinct from standards for grading, which is what is usually meant). What this means is that there is a need for a new—and "higher"—conception of "fundamentals." Everyone, at present, is in favor of having students learn the fundamentals. For most people, "the three R's," or some variation of them, represent what is fundamental to a learner. However, if one *observes* a learner and asks himself, "What is it that this organism needs without which he cannot thrive?," it is impossible to come up with the answer, "The three R's." The "new fundamentals" derive from the emotional and intellectual realities of the human condition, and so "new" answers (well beyond the three-R's type) are possible in response to the question. In *In Defense of Youth,* Earl Kelley lists five such possible answers:

1. the need for other people
2. the need for good communication with other people
3. the need for a loving relationship with other people
4. the need for a workable concept of self
5. the need for freedom.

One does not need to accept all of these in order to accept Kelley's *perspective* on what is fundamental. Obviously, we would want to add to his list "the need to know how to learn," as well as some others which are suggested by our list of "standards" questions. The point is that any curriculum that does not provide for needs as viewed from this perspective— "What does the organism require in order to thrive?"—is not, by our definition, concerned with "fundamentals."

We would like to invite you now to reexamine our sample questions. They represent, after all, a possible curriculum for the new education: The What's-Worth-Knowing Questions Curriculum. This curriculum has several characteristics that require elaboration here. For example, note that all the questions are of a divergent, or open-ended, nature and that each one demands that the learner narrow its focus. Part of the process of learning how to learn is the rephrasing, refining, and dividing of a "worth knowing" question into a series of "answerable worth-knowing questions." It is a fact not easily learned (and almost never in school) that the "answer" to a great many questions is "merely" another question. This is not only true of such questions as we have listed, but even of such questions as "What is a noun?," "Who discovered oxygen?," and "What is the principal river of Uruguay?"

To illustrate the point, we have reproduced below a problem that is sometimes given to students by teachers who regard the process of question asking as basic to education:

1. Study the following questions.
    a. What is the name of this school?

b. Are children of permissive parents more creative than children of nonpermissive parents?

c. Who discovered oxygen?

d. Who is the most beautiful woman in America?

e. Are the people on Mars more advanced than the people on Earth?

f. Will it rain tomorrow?

g. How are you?

h. Will you get into the college of your choice?

i. Is *love* a noun or a verb?

j. $8 + 6 = ?$

k. Why do airplanes crash?

2. Answer the following questions.

a. Which of the questions above can you answer with absolute certainty? How can you be certain of your answer?

b. What information will enable you to answer other questions with absolute certainty? Where will you get the information?

c. Which questions restrict you to giving factual information? Which do not? Which require no facts at all?

d. Which questions require the greatest amount of definition before you try to answer them?

e. Which questions require the testimony of experts? What makes one an expert?

f. Which questions assume the answerer is the expert?

g. Which questions may have false assumptions?

h. Which questions require predictions as answers? What kinds of information may improve the quality of a prediction?

In working this problem through, students quite frequently discover that the question "Who discovered oxygen?" (to cite only one example) is ambiguous in that form. Usually, they rephrase it to read something like, "According to the *Encyclopaedia Britannica*, who is given credit for the 'discovery of oxygen'?" If you feel that there is no important difference between these two questions, or that "everyone knows" that the former implies the latter, may we remind you that, as a matter of fact, the answer to the question "Who discovered

America?" will vary depending on whether you ask it of an Italian, a Swede, or an Irish monk.

Our Questions Curriculum, in addition to requiring the exploration of the nature of questions, has the capacity to *generate* questions that learners are not, at first, aware of. In other words, divergent questions are instruments of "consciousness expansion." They reveal to learners new and relevant areas of inquiry, permitting, quite often, the discovery that one's original question is far less significant than two or three others it has suggested.

Below is a transcript of the first five minutes of an actual lesson conducted in an inquiry mode. In previous lessons the class had inquired into the meanings of the word "right" in three different contexts:

1. It is *right* for a man to give a woman his seat on a bus.
2. It is *right* for children to be vaccinated against polio.
3. It is *right* for citizens to vote.

In this lesson, the students are dealing with the divergent question "What does 'right' mean in statements about language, such as the statement 'It is *right* to say "He doesn't" instead of "He don't." ' " Notice the number of new questions that the students produce in five minutes.

> TEACHER: We have spent a few sessions exploring the shifting meanings of the word "right" in the sentences, 1. It is right for a man to give a woman his seat. 2. It is right for children to be vaccinated. 3. It is right for citizens to vote. Now I have written a fourth sentence on the board, which I would like you to look at: "It is right to say 'he doesn't' instead of 'he don't.' " And what we'll be exploring today is what the "right" means in that sentence. Now who will start us off? You might, if you like, compare its meaning there to its meaning in any of the other sentences.
>
> MARCIA: I think that in that sentence saying "he doesn't" instead of "he don't" that "right" means "accepted." This is what educated people do, or people who have been brought

up well. I think that number 1 about the man giving up his seat is pretty much the same thing.

TEACHER: Are you saying that in sentence 4 we are dealing with a question of etiquette just as we are in sentence 1?

MARCIA: No, it's not exactly etiquette; it's more a reflection of your training and the way you've been brought up. If you've been brought up by hillbillies, you'd probably say "he don't," but if you've been brought up by parents who went to Oxford, you'd say "he doesn't."

TEACHER: O.K. Dan?

DAN: I'd like to ask one question. She said, "If you've been well educated." Who decides who is well educated?

MARCIA: Who decides whether you are well educated? O.K. Well, let me give you a couple of examples! Would you say that someone who had had a sixth-grade education was well educated?

DAN: I wouldn't know.

MARCIA: You wouldn't know?

DAN: It depends on the individual. A person who didn't even go to school but went around the world and just discovered things and read and everything might know more than a person who went to college all his life!

TEACHER: We may have here then right at the beginning a problem with another word. We started out exploring the word "right" and in just three or four minutes of conversation we've come across the word "educated." I think Marcia was suggesting that people who have been to Oxford are educated and hillbillies aren't. Is that what you meant to say?

MARCIA: Well, that's rather the extremes, but yes, more or less.

DAN: Well, you can take a look at our President Lincoln. I don't think he had too much schooling. He had a few private lessons for a couple of years and he was a pretty well edu cated person. His speeches weren't bad. They were well written.

BOB: Most Presidents hire someone to write their speeches, Dan.

DAN: But he didn't. I remember seeing a film on that. He wrote on the train.

TEACHER: On the backs of envelopes, I think. Well, let's get Judy's ideas here.

JUDY: Well, Marcia also said that you speak correctly, but you may be well brought up if you live in slums; your parents might, you know, want to give you what they didn't have and they send you to a good school and things, but still in the house they say "don't" instead of "doesn't" and you most likely will pick up "he don't" instead of "he doesn't."

TEACHER: Well, are you saying, Judy, that one who says "he don't" is not speaking correctly?

JUDY: Maybe in his own home he *is* speaking correctly. It's his accepted way in his own home.

TEACHER: Oh, well now let's stay with this point for a minute. If I interpret what you've said correctly, you are saying that you cannot say that one thing is correct?

JUDY: That's right.

TEACHER: That what may be correct here in our classroom, might not be correct someplace else?

JUDY: Yes, maybe you might say "he doesn't" in school, but when you go home, you say "he don't" because this is how your parents might understand you or someone who lives with you.

TEACHER: Well, Bill, what do you think about this point of view?

BILL: Just because your parents say "he don't" and you say "he don't" in your home, that doesn't make it right. That's just what you do. We do a lot of things that aren't right.

TEACHER: Well, this is what we are trying to find out, Bill. What do we mean by "right" or "correctly"?

BILL: I think in that sentence it means that in the language "he doesn't" are the words that are accepted and used to convey that idea.

TEACHER: Well, who accepts these words and who uses them, and who tells you not to use them?

BILL: The English teachers.

TEACHER: In other words, what English teachers say you should do, becomes right or correct.

BILL: In the classroom, but they get their information from books and other sources.

TEACHER: Well, you have a touching faith in English teachers and I appreciate this. Do you listen to your Social Studies teacher with as much attention as you listen to your English teachers? For example, if the History teacher tells you that a Republican candidate is a better man than some Democratic candidate or vice versa, would you value his judgment as much on that as you would an English teacher's judgment on what's right?

BILL: No, because he's conveying an opinion. The English teacher is telling you a rule that was set down, not by the English teacher, but by somebody else.

TEACHER: Sue, what do you think about this?

SUE: Well, I disagree with him because I think you learn patterns of speech in the years that you are going to elementary school, and when you come up to the junior high and senior high schools, you learn *why* they are right. But the way you learn to talk is taught to you in your early ages. I don't think by the time you're in high school you can change your pattern of speech, because, I mean, they are like different dialects really.

TEACHER: Dialects. What do you understand the word "dialect" to mean?

SUE: Well, like the Southern people might say "you-all" before they start their sentences, and the people in the East won't say this.

TEACHER: They don't say this?

SUE: No.

TEACHER: Well, now, is "you-all" a correct pattern of speech or not?

SUE: Well, perhaps down there it might be, but I don't think it is a correct pattern of speech. I mean I don't really know.

TEACHER: Eric, what do you think?

ERIC: When you spoke of dialects, and you can't change a dialect, my mother came from Richmond, Virginia, and when she came up north she used to say "you-all." She doesn't say that any longer. And now when she goes back to Richmond, Virginia, they all say she has a Northern accent, and she has completely changed her dialect.

SUE: You might be able to pick something up after a while, but I mean like he said you learn how to speak from your English teachers, but you didn't have an English teacher when you were down in—

BILL: I didn't say you learn how to speak. I said you learn the rules that govern how you speak. You learn how to speak when you're a little kid.

RICHARD: I think there have to be some certain rules that are set down by people who think they know what the rules should be. I think in the English language the rules are written in the dictionary and English teachers have followed these rules, and these rules are necessary because, if nobody obeyed the rules, you would not understand what the next person was saying. He might be speaking English, but certainly the rules have to be followed even if you don't like them.

TEACHER: What is your reaction to that? Richard says there must be rules because, if there were not, we could not communicate with each other very well and these rules are written down in books called "dictionaries." Jim?

JIM: These dictionaries—the way people are making it sound as if some small group is sitting in a dark room and they decide how they think about this rule and they decide no we don't like this rule. We will throw it out. Well, this is not the way it is done. The lexicographers sit down and they—

TEACHER: The what?

JIM: The lexicographers.

TEACHER: Let me just put that down. Is that how you spell it, do you know?

JIM: I don't know.

TEACHER [writes on blackboard]: I think that's it, but I think you have to know how to spell it in order to look it up in the dictionary.

JIM: Well, lexicographers. They sit down and they read. They read all the books put out; they read newspapers, magazine articles, speeches; they listen to speeches; they listen to television and radio, and they pick out the way the majority speak. Say they want to see whether you say "he doesn't" or "he don't." They read books, they listen to everything, and they see what the majority uses, and therefore, the dictionary dictates what the majority says.

You noticed, we are sure, that by conventional standards the teacher behaved quite oddly. He had no information to impart and seemed preoccupied with getting the students to question and clarify their own perceptions and statements. Another way of saying this is that the "subject matter" of the lesson was the responses of the learners to the questions they confront. In the next chapter, we shall attempt to explain why *there can never be any other kind of "subject matter" regardless of how the teacher behaves.* Here, we want to point out that at least a half dozen questions were generated by a five-minute discussion of a divergent question and that these questions were produced by the students themselves. These questions include:

1. Who decides what "educated" means?
2. Are English teachers reliable authorities on what constitutes "correct" English?
3. Is there a different standard of "correctness" for each environment?
4. Are dialects "correct"? What is a "dialect"?
5. Are "rules" necessary for communication?
6. What do lexicographers do?

Our "curriculum," when turned over to a group of learners, may therefore, produce 200 further questions. Or, perhaps, a thousand. On one occasion, a group of learners was confronted by the question "What is language?" They transformed this into "What is a language system?" Then, into "What are the characteristics of different language systems or language situations?" After two weeks, the students (with guidance from their teachers) compiled the following list of questions:

On the language of advertising:
What are its purposes? What are its most important symbols? What kinds of relationships does it maintain toward its audiences? What social values does it express? To what extent do these values reflect those of the audience? How do its metaphors work? What are the situations in which its symbolism is most effective? What standards may be used to

judge its truth? In what sense can the language of advertising be "true"?

On the language of news reporting:

What are its purposes? What is "news" anyway? What is a fact? What do we mean by "objectivity"? From whose point of view is news written? How can you tell? What standards may reasonably be used to evaluate news? In what sense can the language of news be said to be "true"?

On the language of politics:

What are its purposes? What are its major assumptions? What are its controlling metaphors? What are its various kinds of statements? What attitudes are required to interpret it intelligently? What is its characteristic tone? What are the meanings of some of its key terms: law, theory, defense, sovereignty, freedom, peace, etc.?

On the language of religion and prayer:

What are the functions of prayer? How does it accomplish its work? What are its rules? How is it organized? From what point of view are religious statements to be evaluated? What are their major assumptions? In what sense can religious statements be said to be true? What are their most important metaphors?

On the language of science:

What are its purposes? What is its characteristic tone? What are its various levels of abstraction? What use does it make of metaphor? From what point of view is it written? What is the meaning of the phrase "scientific truth"? How does it differ from a "religious truth"? From a "political truth"? What standards may be used to evaluate the language of science?

These questions were framed and subsequently answered in an "English" class. But it is fairly obvious that the questions might just as appropriately have been asked in a "social studies" class, or in a course in "anthropology," "linguistics," "semantics," "sociology," "psychology," "theology," "philosophy," "human relations," or "group dynamics." All of which brings us to another characteristic of our questions curriculum: subjects as they are commonly thought of and talked about in schools are rendered less distinct and discrete. They may even disappear.

The first, and less, important reason for this is that it is increasingly difficult to decide what "subjects" to include in a curriculum. Why history and geography? Why not cybernetics and ecology? Why economics and algebra? Why not anthropology and psycho-linguistics? It is difficult to escape the feeling that a conventional curriculum is quite arbitrary in selecting the "subjects" to be studied. The implications of this are worth pondering.

The second, and critical, reason for the breakdown of "subjects" in a new education is more subtle and powerful. Focusing on the asking of questions leads directly to the probing of relationships among "subjects," which, in turn, permits the development of a synoptic and frequently original view of knowledge instead of the traditional segmented view. We have here the crucial difference between a process-oriented perception of knowledge and a static one.

On this point, we find ourselves (regrettably) in disagreement with Jerome Bruner (again). Bruner has advocated a discovery or question-asking approach to teaching in order to help students gain an understanding of what he calls "the structure of the subject." Although there has always been some confusion about exactly what Bruner had in mind with this phrase, it is clear that he sees no reason, when using discovery methods, to abandon the abstraction that is called a "subject." He writes in *The Process of Education*, "The task of teaching a subject to a child at any particular age is one of representing the structure of that subject in terms of the child's way of viewing things." Although he is far too sophisticated to believe it, in this statement and many others like it, Bruner seems to think of a subject as a closed system of finite, fixed, "structured" bits of data. The "subject" is given. It is *there*.

For reasons we have already implied (remember McLuhan on ABCED-minded people?) and which we will elaborate on in the following chapter, this conception of knowledge is much too mechanistic. To begin with, whatever "structure" there is to anything is a product of the cognitive processes of the structurer, i.e., the perceiver, the learner. To quote Heisenberg on this matter: "We have to remember that what we observe is not nature itself, but nature exposed to our methods of questioning." In other words, we do not "get" meanings from our environment. We *assign* meanings. And yet Bruner seems to suggest that there exists in nature a "subject" and that "it" has a "structure." All we then have to do as educators is to find a way of translating the structure that is "out there" so that a child can see "it." But it is clear that the "structure" that is perceived in a "subject" is solely some perceiver's way of viewing things. The structure was made, invented, imagined by a perceiver. If there is one firm conclusion that our intellectual history makes possible, it is stated in the preceding sentence.

We trust that you will not, at this point, accuse us of being solipsistic. We are *not* saying that there isn't anything "out there." We *are* saying that the meaning of what is out there is ascribed to "it" by a perceiver. Thus, a literal translation of the statement of Bruner's we quoted a moment ago would be something like this: "The task of teaching a subject to a child is to make the child perceive objects and relationships the way authorities perceive them." This sounds more like the old education than a new one, especially because it directs the child to see *only* what some previous perceivers have seen. We have already referred to the "discovering your pendulum" application of Bruner's work. The children are taught to "see" exactly what the teacher wants them to see because that is the nature of the "subject." Another name for this is the Seductive Method of Learning. The purpose of this method is identical with that of the old education: to get the learner to "ventriloquize." Ventriloquizing, as Wendell Johnson explained the process, consists essentially of speaking as if with the voice of another —usually an "authority." In school this commonly takes the form of saying back to the teacher what the teacher said or what some book "said." Whatever else this process does, it virtually insures that no thinking (questioning) will occur. Indeed, the penalties for refusing to ventriloquize are elaborate and are ruthlessly invoked.

Of course, in fairness to Bruner, it must be said that he also means by the "structure of a subject" the questions automatically raised in certain "fields." It is certainly true that "historians" ask different kinds of questions from "biologists," and "biologists" from "linguists." But such men are finding, increasingly, that what they thought was someone else's "field" turns out to be theirs as well. We now have mathematical biologists, biophysicists, anthropological psychologists, and so on. They are discovering that the traditional ways of structuring ("seeing") what is out there are both inadequate and arbitrary. As Alan Watts says, the universe is wiggly. Our attempts to take snapshots of the wiggles must not lead us to think that the photograph *is* the wiggle. Besides, someone else may take another photograph and capture an altogether different aspect of the wiggle. And that is exactly what happens when children are allowed to function as question askers and answer seekers. They frequently perceive relationships that others have not noticed before. Let them start with a question in "biology"—for example, "What are the conditions for sustaining life in plants?"—and they will soon start asking questions about "physics," "anthropology," "chemistry," etc. This will happen over and over again unless the teacher insists that they "stick to the subject." But who is to say what the subject is or is not? Besides, the students don't particularly care what *name* is given to the subject. They are engaged in finding things out, in "structuring" what they think they see. And when you are doing that, you have to look where you think there's something to be found. If there's no "official category" for what you're looking at—or for—well, that may even be an advantage. Leeuwenhoek invented the microscope, and the Wright brothers invented the airplane, not knowing that they "couldn't." At least, authorities of their times "knew" and could "prove" that they couldn't. The career of Charles Kettering, one of America's most prolific inventors, is a chronicle of his "doing things that couldn't be done" mostly because he was not suffering from "hardening of the categories." Alfred North Whitehead made the point that taxonomy is the death of science. And, we would add, the memorization of taxonomies is the death of education.

And so in our questions curriculum, "subjects" frequently lose their "clear" and arbitrarily limiting dimensions. We will need to start talking more about the "structure of the learner and his learning" and less about the "structure of the subject."

There are two other characteristics of our questions curriculum that should be mentioned here. The first has to do with that recently discovered (invented?) category of human beings called "disadvantaged children." Generally speaking, these children are reputed to be "slower" learners than other types of children. If this is true, it simply means that they do not function so well as others *in the existing school environment.* It cannot be inferred from this that "disadvantaged children" would be a "problem" if the ecology of the school environment were entirely different. If we may paraphrase Heisenberg: "We have to remember that what we observe children doing in schools is not what they *are,* but children exposed to us by our methods of teaching." We are, in fact, confident that the disadvantaged child is much more likely to find the conditions which will satisfy him as a learner in the kind of environment we have been trying to describe than in any other. In a way, this statement is a tautology since the environment we are describing is devoted to making the learner "satisfied." It is based on what we know about learners, and not on what we know about what we want them to learn.

Finally, note that the questions we listed are capable of being pursued by children at every grade level. Their answers, as well as their *way* of answering, will vary depending on their experience: where they've been, what they believe, and what their purposes are. This curriculum does not call for a single set of answers. Therefore, it does not require a single set of *answerers.* There is an old joke about a school administrator who was dismayed when he and his staff had taken great trouble to prepare a new and wonderful curriculum, only to discover that the "wrong" kids showed up. That's the trouble with the old education and its functionaries: it virtually insures an endless and increasing number of "wrong" students.

It remains for us to say here that the function of the "What's-Worth-Knowing Questions Curriculum" is to put two ideas into clear focus. The first is that the art and science of asking questions is the source of all knowledge. *Any* curriculum of a new education would, therefore, have to be centered around question asking. This means that, even if a school system is unwilling to scrap its present curriculum structure (i.e., "history," "English," "science," etc.), it will need to transform its instructional program so that the major content of what is to be learned by the students results from inquiries structured by the questions that are raised. This implies that students will spend a great deal of their time finding answers to their questions. Question asking and answer finding go hand in hand. And answer finding requires that students go to books, to laboratories, to newspapers, to TV sets, to the streets, to wherever they must go to find their answers.

The second idea is that question asking, if it is not to be a sterile and ritualized activity, has to deal with problems that are perceived as useful and realistic by the learners. We do not mean to suggest that a child's perception of what is relevant is an unalterable given; indeed, the thrust of the "curriculum" we have been describing is to extend the child's perception of what is relevant and what is not.

Simply said: There is no learning without a learner. And there is no, meaning without a meaning maker. In order to survive in a world of rapid change there is nothing more worth knowing, for any of us, than the continuing process of how to make viable meanings.

VI. Meaning Making

WE HAVE BEEN INSISTING that the new education is new, not because it offers *more* of anything, but because it enters into an entirely new "business": fundamentally, the crap-detecting and relevance business. As we have commented, there will be some difficulty persuading teachers that this is their rightful business. But then, teachers have always been somewhat ambivalent about what it is they do for a living. An excellent case in point concerns their conceptions of the human mind. For example, there is the type of teacher who believes he is in the lighting business. We may call him the Lamplighter. When he is asked what he is trying to do with his students, his reply is something like this: "I want to *illuminate* their minds, to allow some light to penetrate the darkness." Then there is the Gardener. He says, "I want to *cultivate* their minds, to fertilize them, so that the seeds I plant will flourish." There is also the Personnel Manager, who wants nothing more than to keep his students' minds busy, to make them efficient and industrious. The Muscle Builder wants to strengthen flabby minds, and the Bucket Filler wants to fill them up.

82

How should we talk about "the human mind" and our always imperfect attempts to do something to it? Shall we put on the lights or dump fertilizer or keep it busy or toughen it up or pump it full? Or maybe we should try, as the Potter does, to mold the mind? Or as the Dietician, to feed it? Or as the Builder, to provide it with a sturdy foundation?

Although we are sorely tempted, it is not our intention to ridicule any of these metaphors of the mind. After all, it is not possible to talk about "the mind" in any terms other than metaphorical. Even the words "the mind" are subtly metaphoric. Think of those words for a moment. Why *the* mind? Why a noun? Why a "thing"? As John Dewey and Arthur Bentley observed, we would come much closer to actuality if we spoke of "minding" (as a process) rather than of "the mind" (as a thing). Obviously, we are using the word "metaphor" to denote any representation of reality, especially linguistic representations. English teachers usually define a metaphor only in a "literary sense." But all language is metaphor to one degree or another. The only reality that is not metaphorical is "reality" itself. All human symbolization, therefore, is metaphor, an abstraction, an "as if." The word is not the thing, Korzybski insisted. Whatever you *say* something is, it is not. Saying something about the world is *not* the world (except perhaps to those whom we call psychotic). The rest of us always wrestle with the question "What words shall we use to represent 'things'?" The problem is complicated by the fact that "things" are so damned wiggly. And further by the fact that almost nothing is more wiggly than the process of "minding." In the next chapter we shall deal explicitly with the role of "languaging" in the new education. Here we want to say that the Lamplighter, the Gardener, and the rest are merely doing what anyone must do in order to "think" about "minding." But in saying this, we have not closed the matter. We have opened it. For example, are there metaphors of the mind that come closer to actuality than others? Does the new education rely heavily on a particular metaphor? And what difference does it make?

The answer to the first question is quite obviously yes. Increasingly, there is a sense among psychologists, psychiatrists, psycho-linguists, physicists, and even theologians that the various "thing" metaphors of the mind are inept and misleading. They imply a static and segmented "entity" codified in a system of polarized categories that hardly seem to represent what really happens when we think or learn or act. There are "the emotions," "the intellect," "the spirit," "the I.Q." There is "smartness" and "dumbness," "discipline" and "instruction," as if there were things inside of us that corresponded to one or the other. We find ourselves making such statements as, "The school will deal with the child's intellect, the home with his emotions, the church with his spirit." (And the hospital with his liver?)

But it would appear that, in spite of the categories, people "happen" as wholes in process. Their "minding" processes are simultaneous functions, not discrete compartments. You have never met anyone who was "thinking," who was not at the same time also "emoting," "spiritualizing," and for that matter, "livering." When the old progressive educationists spoke of teaching "the whole child," they were not being idealistic. They were being descriptive. Teachers have no other alternative than to teach "the whole child." The fact that teachers exclude "the emotions" and "the spirit" from their lessons does not, of course, mean that those processes are unaffected by what the teacher does. Plato said that, in order for education to accomplish its purpose, reason must have an adequate emotional base, and Dewey spoke often of "collateral learning," by which he meant most of the learnings that occur while the teacher is dealing with "the intellect." Naturally, these are the most enduring learnings, probably because they are not programmed, syllabused, tested, and graded. The effect of the teacher's isolation of the "intellect" is that certain important features of human beings tend to go unnoticed. For example, the curricula of most schools—especially those most single-mindedly pursuing "the intellect"—do not seem to recognize the fact that boys are different from girls. This is exceedingly odd, since almost everybody else has noticed differences. For another example, the curricula of many urban schools do not reveal any awareness of differences between white, middle-class children and black, nonmiddle-class children. And the price we all pay for this omission in incalculable.

We trust that these observations do not come as a revelation to you. It is difficult to imagine that many serious people believe that "the emotions," "the intellect," "the spirit," or, for that matter, "the id," "ego," and "superego" are very much more than metaphors with quite limited utility. And yet it seems to be extremely difficult for us to part with them or refrain from inventing new and equally static ones. The structure of our language is relentless in forcing upon us "thing" conceptions. In English, we can transform any process or relationship into a "thing" by the simple expedient of naming "it" into a noun. We have done this with "rain" and "explosions," with "waves" and "clouds," with "thought" and "life." Professor Allen Walker Read in researching the origin and uses of the word "psychosomatic" provides us with a recent example. The word was evidently coined to express a relationship and a process, explicitly to *deter* us from thinking that illness can always be categorized as either physical or mental. What happened is typical. We began to use "psychosomatic" as a synonym for "mental." ("Give it to me straight, Doc. Am I sick or is it only psychomatic?")

Even the term "the whole child," in spite of its good intentions, is as static a metaphor as any of the others. "Child" is a "thing" word, and there is no stage of human growth that is more visibly a process than "childhood."

It is as if nouns battle verbs for dominance as our seminal metaphors. The nouns mostly win. Or *have* won, up to now. Marshall McLuhan implies that the dominance of the noun metaphor is, to a considerable extent, a function of an ABCED-minded, alphabetic-writing, and print-oriented culture. With the advent of electricity and electronic media, process metaphors seem to be increasing in currency and may, in the end, prevail. A "happening" is a process metaphor. So is a "be-in," "taking a trip," "cooling it" and "making the scene." This last one is especially significant, as we will try to show in a moment when explaining the metaphor of the mind that we prefer. Suffice it to say here that there is increasing evidence that we "make" the reality we perceive rather than passively "receive" or "reflect" it. It is also significant, we think, that the process metaphors we have just mentioned are mostly derived from the language of young people, who are, after all, our first full-fledged electronic-media generation and who comprise, for the first time ever, about half of our total population. It is only slightly speculative to say that one of the reasons they have "turned off" and "tuned out" their educational experience is that the machine-age categories of school systems seem to them arbitrary, unrealistic, stifling, and altogether antagonistic to anyone who insists on his right to use the widest range of his senses. There are "the courses," "the midterms," "the finals," "the term paper," "the subjects," "the A's, B's, and C's." There's Geography on Monday, History on Tuesday, Civics on Wednesday. One hears incessantly, "Line up in size places," "Boys on one side, girls on the other" (one of the few notices taken of the difference between boys and girls in school), "Get in alphabetical order," and "We won't get to that question for another two weeks." What can't be graded doesn't exist, and what can doesn't seem important. There are little spontaneity and genuine dialogue, and no sense of the simultaneity of experience. There is certainly no opportunity for intense involvement of "the whole child." In a word, reality, as the young perceive it, is missing. The kids who finally, in quiet desperation, "split the scene" may unwittingly be telling us, through their metaphor, that it's the damned *sequences, lines, compartments,* and *categories* that need to be split, rearranged, and integrated.

It seems fairly evident that our youth are suspicious of how we have divided and sliced reality with our linguistic categories. They resent being "put in a bag," especially someone else's "bag." We need hardly say that all of this is extremely serious in its consequences, as any conflict between seminal metaphors always is. What we have here is not "merely" a dispute over what names we shall use for "things," but more fundamentally, a dispute over which "things" are to be named. The structure of our language is not neutral in the dispute. As we have said, it has tended to favor the "fixed categories" people as against "the process and relationship" people.

Our language prejudices us in still another way. Our sentence structure is predisposed to the idea that each of us is separate and distinct from what is outside of our skins. We alluded to this belief in the previous chapter—the idea that reality is independent of us, that we play no role in "making the scene." It is very difficult to escape from this idea as long as we are confined to conventional language. Even in the simplest sentence, such as "I see you," there is an implicit suggestion that what *I* am doing is independent of *you*, like the teacher who "teaches" whether or not the student is "learning," or the seller who "sells" whether or not the customer is "buying." Of course, it is relatively easy for most of us to accept the idea that "teaching-learning" or "selling-buying" are *transactions* (processes) and not discrete, separate events. It is more difficult to accept the idea that the process of my seeing you is also a psychological and symbolic transaction. The standard reply to such an idea is, "You mean to say that the person you 'see' is not really *there*, that the perceiver has 'made him up'?" The answer is simultaneously yes and no. We start with the assumption that there are "things" outside of our skin. But how do we "see" those things? Well, one might say, "You just *look*." But look at what? And how? And what do we mean by "looking"? And how is it that two people "look" at the "same thing" and "see" different things? Scientists, particularly, are becoming increasingly aware that what anything "is" depends on how who looks at what.

We hope you will agree that these are important questions, since the fundamental metaphor of the mind of the new education is based on the most recent answers to them. The metaphor we are referring to is the title of this chapter: "minding" as "meaning making." Before explaining what are the implications of this conception of the mind, we want to acknowledge where it comes from. Such acknowledgment must begin with Adelbert Ames, Jr. (And *who*, everybody asks, is Adelbert Ames, Jr.?) Unlike Marshall McLuhan, he never captured the attention of the press or intellectuals, and it is safe to say that not one teacher in 5,000 has ever heard his name. Yet, it is doubtful that any "educationist" of recent times has more impressive credentials. In the first paragraph of his first published letter to Ames (in December 1946), John Dewey wrote:

> It would not be possible for me to overstate my judgment as to the importance of your demonstrations with respect to visual perception nor the importance of their being widely known. While the demonstrations themselves are in the field of visual perception, they bear upon the entire scope of psychological theory and upon all practical applications of psychological knowledge, beginning with education.

In his last published letter to Ames (in November 1950), Dewey wrote, "I think your work is by far the most important work done in the psychological-philosophical field during this century—I am tempted to say the *only* really important work." (Dewey's italics.)

Alfred North Whitehead called Ames an "authentic genius." And Horace Kallen compared him to Leonardo. So how come no one knows about him? Partly, we suppose, because Ames did not write a book. With a print-minded intellectual class, this deficiency is virtually an insurmountable obstacle to recognition. Perhaps another reason is that Ames was exceedingly tentative in setting forth his findings. His tentativeness was consistent with the substance of his work, but it could not have been attractive to the press and other mass media. A third reason might well be that the results of Ames' work are truly revolutionary and, we think, staggering in their implications for education. Nobody likes a smart revolutionary, especially an amateur. And an "amateur" Ames certainly was. Here are the bare facts:

He was born in 1880. He graduated from Harvard, practiced law, later studied art, and painted for a number of years. His interest in art led to an interest in physiological optics, and he obtained a research fellowship at Clark University which he held until World War I. After the war, Ames went to Dartmouth as a research professor, first in the Department of Physiological Optics, and then in the Dartmouth Eye Institute, which he established. He died in 1955, largely unknown to the people who could profit most by his work, namely, teachers.

Beginning in 1938, Ames created a series of "demonstrations" designed to study the nature of perception. His "laboratory" included oddly shaped rooms, chairs, windows and other objects which seemed to "distort" reality when perceived by ordinary people. Perhaps his most impressive "demonstration" is the trapezoidal window which revolved in a 360° circle. The perceiver, however, observes that the window turns 180°, stops, and then turns back 180°. Some of the people who were shown the "demonstrations" were not convinced that they had any significance and labeled them "optical illusions." But a few thought otherwise, including Albert Einstein, Dewey, Hadley Cantril, and Earl Kelley. Dewey believed that Ames had provided empirical evidence for the "transactional psychology" he and Arthur Bentley had formulated in Knowing and the Known. This term was used by them to minimize the mechanistic oversimplification caused by the use of the term "interaction." The sense of "transactional psychology" is that what human beings are and what they make their environment into is a product of a mutually simultaneous, highly complex, and continuing "bargaining" process between what is inside their skins and outside. Dewey believed that Ames had provided substantial understandings of the nature of that bargaining process.

Cantril sensed that Ames' work had great significance for social psychology and developed the point in his book The "Why" of Man's Experience. Kelley saw at once the meanings of the demonstrations for education. In his book Education for What Is Real (with an introduction by Dewey), he describes Ames' experiments in detail, and suggests how these studies in perception, if understood and applied, would change the schooling process. In our judgment, it is the best "education" book written in the past 20 years and probably one of the least known. What is it that Ames seemed to prove? The first and most important fact uncovered by his perception studies is that *we do not get our perceptions from the "things" around us. Our perceptions come from us.* This does *not* mean that there is nothing outside of our skins. It does mean that whatever is "out there" can never be known except as it is filtered through a human nervous system. We can never get outside of our own skins. "Reality" is a perception, located somewhere behind the eyes.

Secondly, it seems clear from the Ames studies that what we perceive is largely a function of our previous experiences, our assumptions, and our purposes (i.e., needs). In other words, the perceiver decides what an object is, where it is, and why it is according to his purpose and the assumptions that he makes at any given time. You tend to perceive what you want and need to perceive, and what your past experience has led you to assume will "work" for you.

Third, we are unlikely to alter our perceptions until and unless we are frustrated in our attempts to do something based on them. If our actions seem to permit us to fulfill our purposes, we will not change our perceptions no matter how often we are told that they are "wrong." In fact, the meaning of "wrong" in this context is a perception that does not "work" for the perceiver. This does *not* mean, however, that we automatically change our perceptions if we are frustrated in our attempts to act on them. This does mean that we have available the alternative of changing our perceptions. The ability to learn can be seen as the ability to relinquish inappropriate perceptions and to develop new—and more workable—ones.

Fourth, since our perceptions come from us and our past experience, it is obvious that each individual will perceive what is "out there" in a unique way. We have no common world, and communication is possible only to the extent that two perceivers have similar purposes, assumptions, and experience. The process of becoming an effective social being is contingent upon seeing the other's point of view.

Fifth, perception is, to a much greater extent than previously imagined, a function of the linguistic categories available to the perceiver. As we said, reality is a perception located somewhere behind the eyes. But "behind the eyes" there is a language process. We know that "nature" never repeats or standardizes. We do it. And how we do it depends on the categories and classifications of our language system. It is only a slight exaggeration to say we "see" with our language.

Sixth, the meaning of a perception is how it causes us to *act*. If rain is falling from the sky, some people will head for shelter, others will enjoy walking in it. Their perceptions of "what is happening" are different as reflected in the fact that they "do" different things. The fact that both groups will agree to the sentence "It is raining" does not mean they perceive the "event" in the same way.

In the light of all this, perhaps you will understand why we prefer the metaphor "meaning making" to most of the metaphors of the mind that are operative in the schools. It is, to begin with, much less static than the others. It stresses a process view of minding, including the fact that "minding" is undergoing constant change. "Meaning making" also forces us to focus on the individuality and the uniqueness of the meaning *maker* (the *minder*). In most of the other metaphors there is an assumption of "sameness" in all learners. The "garden" to be cultivated, the darkness to be lighted, the foundation to be built upon, the clay to be molded—there is always the implication that all learning will occur in the same way. The flowers will be the same color, the light will reveal the same room, the clay will take the same shape, and so on. Moreover, such metaphors imply boundaries, a limit to learning. How many flowers can a garden hold? How much water can a bucket take? What happens to the learner after his mind has been molded? How large can a building be, even if constructed on a solid foundation? The "meaning maker" has no such limitations. There is no end to his educative process. He continues to create new meanings, to make new transactions with his environment.

We come then to the question "What difference does it all

make?" It seems clear to us that, if teachers *acted* as if their students were meaning makers, almost everything about the schooling process would change. For example, most school practices are based on the assumption that the student is fundamentally a *receiver*, that the object ("subject matter") from which the stimulus originates is all-important, and that the student has no choice but to see and understand the stimulus as "it" is. We now know that this assumption is false. To quote Earl Kelley:

> Now it comes about that whatever we tell the learner, he will make something that is all his own out of it, and it will be different from what we held so dear and attempted to "transmit." He will build it into his own scheme of things, and relate it uniquely to what he already uniquely holds as experience. Thus he builds a world all his own, and what is really important is what he makes of what we tell him, not what we intended.

In other words, you end up with a "student-centered curriculum" not because it is good for "motivation" but because you don't, in fact, have any other choice.

There is no such thing as "subject matter" in the abstract. "Subject matter" exists in the minds of perceivers. And what each one thinks it is, is what it is. We have been acting in schools as if knowledge lies outside the learner, which is why we have the kinds of curricula, syllabi, and texts we have. But knowledge, as Kelley points out, is what we know *after* we have learned. It is an outcome of perception and is as unique and subjective as any other perception. Thus, if you assume you are confronted by a "meaning maker" rather than an "empty bucket," you would quite logically stop the practice of preparing and using syllabi and texts which state exactly what knowledge is to be learned. You would certainly not expect that the "same" knowledge is to be learned by every student. Indeed, you would feel that such an occurrence would be most undesirable, even if possible, which it is not. You would resent "standardized" examinations which devalue, even denigrate, the uniqueness of each learner's perceptions. You would never be able to say what your "class" has learned, since there is no such "thing" as a "class," only 22 or 34 or 43 individual perceivers. Your entire system of evaluation would have to be scrapped. How would you know whose perceptions to value most, and whose least?

There is a sad little joke about a fifth-grade teacher in a ghetto school who asked a grim Negro boy, during the course of a "science" lesson, "How many legs does a grasshopper have?" "Oh, man," he replied, "I sure wish I had *your* problems!" Would you penalize the boy for having different purposes from his teacher and, therefore, for his valuing and perceiving a different reality? And on what grounds would you assign a "higher grade" to one perceiver over another? Because one has shared the teacher's perception of "knowledge" whereas the "dumb" perceiver has not? Your methods of instruction would be turned inside out. You would refrain practically entirely from lecturing, since a lecture is based on the assumption that its "content" is what is to be learned. But a "lecture" is only what you said from your point of view. For the learner, its content is what *he heard*. And so you would have to work continually to find out what the learner heard, which means you would be abandoning lecturing for the rest of the year. You would have to revise completely your procedures for "grouping" students and especially your methods of labeling and defining their potential. As we were writing these words, an almost perfect example of the necessity for this appeared on the front page of *The New York Times* (August 8, 1967). Below is the headline and the first four paragraphs:

STUDY INDICATES PUPILS DO WELL
WIIEN TEACHER IS TOLD THEY WILL

by John Leo

Four years ago Robert Rosenthal, now a 34-year-old professor of social psychology at Harvard, reported after tests that rats performed far better when the experimenters were told, falsely, that the rats had been specially bred for intelligence.

The same kind of rats consistently turned in poor performances when the experimenters had been told the animals were
dull, he said.

Professor Rosenthal then began similar tests on schoolchildren, with what he termed similar results. A random sample
of first- and second-grade children at a South San Francisco
elementary school, who it was predicted would make dramatic
gains in schoolwork, actually made those gains, while the rest
of the student body did not. Only the teachers and not the
pupils or parents had been told of the predictions.

Although, for ethical reasons, it was not predicted that any
child would turn out dull, Professor Rosenthal believes that
his tests provide important evidence supporting the common
thesis that many children, particularly minority-group children,
turn out dull because their teachers expect them to be dull.*

Perhaps the most interesting feature of this story is that it
appeared on the front page of *The New York Times.* The fact
that the editors believed that such an "obvious" learning occurrence was so newsworthy is evidence of how tragically inept
are most of our metaphors of the mind. How many children
do you suppose have been driven to stupidity because their
teachers believed that they "really" were "stupid"? The story
says that Dr. Rosenthal declined, *for ethical reasons,* to estab-
lish groups of "dumb" children. Yet, there is hardly a school in
the country that has not organized children into groups labeled
"dumb" so that both their teachers and they can know exactly
what they "are." In other words, using the metaphor "meaning
makers" would help us to abandon our notions of "fixed intelligence," which in turn would weaken almost all of our reasons
for grouping children and labeling them. The research cited
in *The Times* should make every teacher who tells a parent
that his child is not "capable" of learning somewhat ashamed
of himself. At the same time, it is difficult to blame such teachers. The metaphors of the mind they have adopted as the basis
of their procedures cannot explain to them what Dr. Rosen-

* For a detailed discussion of these experiments see *Pygmalion in the
Classroom* by Rosenthal and Jacobson.

thal discovered, and perhaps they do not believe that such things can happen. A bucket does not get bigger simply by saying it will. Neither does a foundation become sturdier, nor a garden more luxuriant. Therefore, it is worth spending a moment to comment on what seems to have happened in Dr. Rosenthal's studies.

There are, to begin with, two different "events" that have occurred. One of them is best illustrated by the reference to the rats which appeared to behave intelligently, according to the perceptions of experimenters who were told that the rats were specially bred for intelligence. Did the rats "actually" behave intelligently? We can assume that the rats were behaving neither "intelligently" nor "stupidly." They were just behaving. Whether such behavior is intelligent or stupid has less to do with the behavior than it does with a human perception and evaluation of that behavior. What happened was this: The experimenters, having classified the rats as "intelligent," selected those "bits" of behavior, those wiggles, that would be consistent with the label. They "saw" intelligent behavior because that is what they expected to see. Experimenters "looking" at rats they believed to be dull saw "dull" behavior for the same reason. What we "see" is a product of what we believe to be "out there." We see things not as "they" are, but as we are.

The case of the elementary-school children is quite similar, but with an additional dimension. The teachers "perceived" these children as intelligent because they were expecting to see "intelligent behavior." The teachers, like the laboratory experimenters, "made" the reality that was "there." But we can assume that once the teachers "made" that reality, the children began to "make" one of their own. The children modified their behavior in accordance with the positive expectations of their teachers. In other words, the children changed their perceptions of themselves, and they did so because their environment had a positive effect on their purposes and assumptions. The report does not give the details of that environment, except the part that concerns the attitude of the teachers. Nonetheless, there is every reason to suppose that in an inquiry environment the process of positive perception change occurs more efficiently than in any other, if only because it minimizes negative teacher response. Look back (to Chapter V) at the five-minute excerpt from an inquiry lesson and you will find all the reasons. The teacher has obviously not assumed that knowledge lies outside the learner; therefore, he does not need to "get" anything "inside" the heads of the students. Moreover, there is nothing that the learner can say that is "irrelevant." What would it be irrelevant to? Certainly not the learner. If the teacher were to observe that a certain observation is "beside the point," how would that change the student's perception? It would mainly have the effect of making the learner feel inadequate, that he cannot quite understand what the lesson is about. But in an inquiry environment, the lesson is always *about* the learner. He is "the content." It is about the meanings he has in his head (including the meanings about himself as a learner), and the possibility of his modifying and extending those meanings.

From an entirely different direction, confirmation of the educational implications of Ames' studies is provided by the work of I. A. Richards. His investigations offer detailed descriptions of the complexities of the process of meaning making. The transactional nature of this process is dramatically illustrated by Richards' descriptions of what happens when readers confront a printed page. Richards has been insisting for over 40 years that the "study of literature" is a rather pointless and, in fact, nonexistent activity. What one can study are the *meanings* readers assign to literary works. What people call "literature" does not exist on paper. The only thing you will ever find on paper are black marks. The meanings assigned to these black marks are what we may call the "literary experience," and *that* is what Richards has studied. His book *Practical Criticism* is a catalogue of meanings that different readers assigned to certain black marks on paper. Richards tries to explain the processes by which these meanings were produced, and suggests ways in which "teachers" can help readers to modify their perceptions. Richards presents certain criteria for meaning making in reading. At no point does Richards say that any meaning is just as "good" as any other. Since our perceptions come from the past, it is possible to ascribe anything we desire to the clues we receive. Obviously, we need to have some procedures for determining the reliability of a perception. For example, we need to be able to distinguish the difference between a psychopathic statement and a scientific one. In the next chapter we will discuss in some detail such criteria. The point being made here is that, *whatever criteria you use*, all you ever have to work with, as a teacher, are the perceptions of learners at a particular time. Thus, Richards' lessons in "literature" are always lessons about the meanings his students make and why they feel these meanings are the most appropriate they can make. That was exactly the approach of the teacher in the inquiry lesson in Chapter V. The lesson was about the meanings his students gave to "correct English" and why, and if they felt these meanings were the most useful available. That is all any lesson can ever be about. The inquiry environment simply recognizes that fact, proceeds from it, and uses it to extend the range of viable alternatives.

As soon as students realize that their lessons are about *their* meanings, then the entire psychological context of schools is different. Learning is no longer a contest between them and something outside of them, whether the problem be a poem, a historical conclusion, a scientific theory, or anything else. There is, then, no need for the kinds of "motivation" found in the conventional Trivia contest. There are few occasions for feelings of inadequacy, few threats to their sense of dignity, less reason to resist changing perceptions. In short, the meaning-maker metaphor puts the student at the center of the learning process. It makes both possible and acceptable a plurality of meanings, for the environment does not exist only to impose standardized meanings but rather to help students improve their unique meaning-making capabilities. And this is the basis of the process of learning how to learn, how to deal with the otherwise "meaningless," how to cope with change that requires new meanings to be made.

VII. Languaging

IT IS NOT TOO UNCOMMON in the history of the human group for a simple idea to change the entire direction of life in a society. Consider, for example, the idea that the earth revolves around the sun rather than vice versa. Or the idea of evolution, or that a man may govern only by the consent of the governed. Most often, ideas of this type do not change everything immediately. It takes a while. Sometimes a war or two. But in the end, the idea prevails, and nothing is the same as it was before.

We are not alone in thinking that the idea that our perceptions come from us, that we "see" things not as *they* are but as *we* are, has a potency similar in magnitude to the Copernican conception of the universe. Copernicus' idea turned the universe inside out. It removed man from its center where he had instinctively placed himself, and put him on the periphery, and then on the periphery of a periphery. The idea of man as a meaning maker puts him back at the center of the universe, although not in the same sense as before.

We now know that each man creates his own unique world,

that he, and he alone, generates whatever reality he can ever know. But this is not exactly a cause for unqualified celebration. It turns out, for example, that John Donne was wrong. Each man *is* an island entire of itself. The purposes and assumptions and, therefore, the perceptions of each man are uniquely his, and there is no one else in the vast sea of the universe who shares them in every detail. Among other things, this means that no man can be absolutely certain of anything. The best anyone can ever do is to say how something appears to *him*. The cosmos offers no absolute confirmations. Relativity and the uncertainty principle are more—much more—than technical terms in physics. Each one of us must live with them every second of our lives.

It turns out, too, that language is far from being neutral in the process of perceiving, as well as in the process of evaluating perceptions. We have been accustomed to thinking that language "expresses" thought and that it "reflects" what we see. We now know that this belief is naïve and simplistic, that our languaging process is fully implicated in any and all of our attempts to assess reality. As studies in perception indicate, we do not "get" meaning from things, we assign meaning. But beyond this, there is a growing understanding that the meaning we assign is a function of the pattern or system of symbols through which we order and relate whatever it is we are dealing with. In other words, whatever is out there isn't anything until we make it something, and then it "is" whatever we make it. Most of our "making something" activity, of course, consists essentially of naming things. Korzybski reminded us that whatever we say something is, it is not. But in a certain sense, whatever we say something is, it is. Because we have said it, and because of having said it, we will perceive it as such. Another way of saying this is that, once we have taken snapshots of the wiggles that comprise the universe, the snapshots become our reality. Is it not true that we believe that time consists of a past, a present, and a future? That time is segmented into units of days, months, and years? That the world is made up of separate bits of things? That things have inherent characteristics? That a thing is either A or not A, and that it can never be both at the same time? Such beliefs as these we now know are consequences of our language system, of our methods of codifying reality, and may or may not bear much resemblance to the wiggles outside of our skin.

One of our favorite examples of the extent to which people can be unaware of the role that language plays in their assessment of reality occurred in the year 1752, when the British government instituted a calendar reform. The measure required that September 2 of that year be dated September 14. The result was that many people imagined that they had been deprived of eleven days in their lives. Their confusion was somewhat analogous to that of the man who, upon being told that it was 90° outside, said, "No wonder it's so hot!" A more common example of our language habits producing perceptions is in the process known as "projection." "Projection," as the term is used by semanticists such as Korzybski and Hayakawa, means that we transfer our own feelings and evaluations to objects outside of us. For example, we say, "John is stupid" or "Helen is smart," as if "stupidity" and "smartness" were characteristics of John and Helen. A literal translation of "John is stupid" (that is, its most scientific meaning) might go something like this: "When I perceive John's behavior, I am disappointed or distressed or frustrated or disgusted. The sentence I use to express *my* perceptions and evaluation of these events is 'John is stupid.'"

When we say, "John is stupid," we are talking about ourselves much more than we are talking about John. And yet, this fact is not reflected at all in the statement. The *I*—the involvement of the perceiver—has been removed by a grammatical peculiarity. Our grammar has forced us to "objectify" our feelings, to project them onto something outside of our skins. "Stupidity" is a grammatical category. It does not exist in "nature." Yet we imagine that it does because our language has put it there.

This point of view about language and reality has sometimes been called the "Sapir-Whorf Hypothesis." The reference is to

Edward Sapir and his student Benjamin Lee Whorf, both of whom were anthropologists with a special interest in the operations of language. Their studies of the language systems of different cultures led them to the conclusion (Whorf more than Sapir) that each language—including both its structure and its lexicon—represents a unique way of perceiving reality. They believed that we are imprisoned, so to speak, in a house of language. We try to assess what is outside the house from our position within it. However, the house is "oddly" shaped (and no one knows precisely what a "normal" shape would be). There is a limited number of windows. The windows are tinted and are at odd angles. We have no choice but to see what the structure of the house permits us to see.

No doubt, you will recognize that the Sapir-Whorf Hypothesis (sometimes also called the "Sapir-Whorf-Korzybski Hypothesis") is a restatement of the proposition that the "medium is the message," since it maintains that the medium (in this case, one's language) not only structures what one will see and believe, but is, in fact, inseparable from what one sees and believes. This perspective of the role of language in perception has been called a "hypothesis" largely because it has been extremely difficult to design precise experiments which would either "prove" or "disprove" it. Nonetheless, in almost every field of learning—for example, physics, linguistics, philosophy, psychology, medicine—this "hypothesis" has gained wide acceptance. In fact, we may now refer to it as "The Sapir-Whorf-Korzybski-Ames-Einstein-Heisenberg-Wittgenstein-McLuhan-Et Al. Hypothesis." For those of you who are especially interested in the "Et Al.," we have included an appendix to this chapter, consisting entirely of quotations from those, past and present, who accept in *one degree or another* the view that language is not merely a vehicle of expression, it is also the driver; and that what we perceive, and therefore can learn, is a function of our languaging processes. What these quotations mean, coming as they do from men of such distinction in diverse areas of human activity, is this: In the new education, language assumes an importance that it has not previously had in any educational philosophy. One would have to go back to the trivium to find a comparable emphasis, but as we hope to show, we would propose going far beyond that.

To begin with, we are in a position to understand that almost all of what we customarily call "knowledge" is language. Which means that the key to understanding a "subject" is to understand its language. In fact, that is a rather awkward way of saying it, since it implies that there is such a thing as a "subject" which contains "language." It is more accurate to say that what we call a subject *is* its language. A discipline" is a way of knowing, and whatever is known is inseparable from the symbols (mostly words) in which the knowing is codified. What is biology (for example) other than words? If all the words that biologists use were subtracted from the language, there would be no "biology." Unless and until new words were invented. Then, we would have a "new" biology. What is "history" other than words? Or astronomy? Or physics? If you do not know the meanings of "history words" or "astronomy words," you do not know history or astronomy. This means, of course, that every teacher is a language teacher. We do not mean this in the sense that is implied when a principal reminds his Science, Math, and Social Studies teachers that they are also English teachers. The principal usually means that he wants everyone to check for spelling, punctuation, and grammar on the papers that students hand in. We mean that Biology, Math, and History teachers, quite literally, have little else to teach but a way of talking and therefore seeing the world. The new English, the new Math, the new Social Studies represent new languages. And a new language inevitably means new possibilities of perception.

For this reason, the new education, in addition to being student-centered and question-centered must also be language-centered. And here at the risk of laboring the point, we must say that by "language-centered" we do *not* mean what the English teachers are apt to mean by the phrase: that instead of emphasizing literature in the classroom, one should emphasize the study of grammar, language history, and regional dialects. Perhaps you have sensed that we harbor a particularly acute hostility toward many English teachers. Our reason has to do with their relentless trivialization of the study of language in the schools. Dolphins aside, man is the only languaging creature on the planet. What does that mean? For the "worst" English teachers, it has meant teaching sentence diagramming, the parts of speech, the difference between "who" and "whom," and Shakespeare. For the "best," it has meant teaching composition, the history of the language, modern literature, and the new grammars. We might call all of this—the best and the worst—the cosmetic approach to language, a view of language which sees it primarily as an instrument of upward social mobility. It is almost impossible to find language studied as *the major factor in producing our perceptions, our judgments, our knowledge, and our institutions.* The new education proposes such a study of language, as I. A. Richards intended in the following quote from *Interpretation in Teaching:*

> There are trivial ways of studying language which have no connection with life, and these we need to clear out of our schools. But a deeper and more thorough study of our use of words is at every point a study of our ways of living. It touches all the modes of interpretive activity—in techniques, and in social intercourse—upon which civilization depends.

Indeed it does, and for the remainder of this chapter we would like to indicate some of the concepts and strategies that would comprise a "thorough study" of language in the schools. We need hardly say that such study need not be confined to an "English" class. In fact, since "English" classes generally are not about anything in reality, they are unlikely places for meaningful inquiries into language and reality to occur. As Wendell Johnson said, you can't write writing. You have to write *about* something. The same is true of speaking, listening, reading, inquiring; in short, all languaging activity. The meaningful study of language, in other words, must be about the relationship of language to reality, whether the "subject" is history, politics, biology, religion, war, or anything else. In this way, the student can begin to develop standards by which he can judge the value of perceptions—his own or anyone else's. As Richards points out, the study of language is the study of our ways of living, which is to say our ways of perceiving reality. Granted that each man's perceptions are unique, we still need to know if someone's statements about the world are "better" than someone else's. We need to have ways of telling the difference between a lunatic and a scientist, and of distinguishing among all the possibilities in between. We need to have methods of differentiating a "good" answer from a "bad" one, a workable solution from a failure. This is, after all, the business of a competent crap detector. Thus, it is entirely appropriate for the new education to seek assistance from one of the most vigorous crap detectors of our age. We are referring to Alfred Korzybski.

Korzybski was a Polish-born engineer whose experience in World War I provoked him into attempting to lay the foundations for a "science of man." His focus from the start was the role of language in human affairs and how it simultaneously enabled man to "bind time" while it blinded him to his own time. In 1933, with the publication of *Science and Sanity*, Korzybski set forth what he called his "science of General Semantics." Korzybski was convinced that man's nonscientific use of language increasingly insulated him from reality and therefore diminished his prospect of survival. As a consequence, he devised a system of language strategies intended to keep language users conscious of the degree to which their language corresponded, or did not correspond, to something capable of sense verification. In a way, all scientific activity can be viewed as "semantic verification" in Korzybski's sense. Science, which is an extension and refinement of man's ability to perceive "reality," requires that we talk, and hence think, differently about what is going on around us. This kind of talking has always caused a great deal of distress among those who have become enamored of certain words and combinations of words (ideas). The history of science is a chronicle of the unhappy responses that have occurred when someone, somewhere, has pointed out that what everyone had been saying and believing up to that point is nonsense.

Before indicating some of the major concepts of Korzybski, we think it worth saying that Korzybski predated McLuhan by many years in developing the point that the medium is the message. When Korzybski observed that the "word is not the thing," or "whatever we say something is, it is not," or when he discussed the effects of projection and of the different and unconscious uses of "is," he was essentially saying that the form of language was its most critical content. It is the form of our utterances, he insisted, that works us over, "massages" us, and all the more so because of our being unaware of it. Language is our most profound and possibly least visible environment. Whether one says, "John is stupid" or "John is brilliant," Korzybski observed, is a less important message than the message that is contained in the form of the statement itself, namely, that "stupidity" or "brilliance" is a characteristic of John. Had Korzybski been as skillful a punster and phrase maker as McLuhan, he might have had a more dazzling impact on the intellectual community. As it was, his verbal play took the form of such observations as "Categorical and dogmatic thinking are more suitable to cats and dogs than to human beings." It might be said, however, that insofar as education is concerned, Korzybski and McLuhan (and Ames and Richards and Wiener and Heisenberg and Einstein et al.) have had about equal impact: zero. In Korzybski's case, this fact is particularly distressing since, more than any of the others save Dewey, he was explicitly an educationist. His general seman tics is a reeducational system whose purpose is to train people to use language as scientists do when they are being scientific. This is done through the application of various tactics intended to raise the effects of the languaging process to a conscious level and to keep such awareness relatively constant.

What are some of the specific kinds of awareness Korzybski's system is intended to develop?

First, and probably central to all the others, is the awareness that meaning is not "in" words. Meaning is in people, and whatever meanings words have are assigned or ascribed to them by people. We have already alluded to this concept, calling it "projection." It is important to recognize that people cannot give, assign, or ascribe meanings which they do not already have in their experience. Obviously, a word and its referent that are beyond one's experience are "meaningless." Thus, to talk about what words mean rather than what people mean obscures rather than clarifies the relationship between language and reality.

A second concept, closely related to the first, is the awareness that words are not what they ostensibly refer to. Or, as it is usually put, "the word is not the thing." This concept seems so "obvious" that it hardly seems worth stating. (Bear in mind, though, Whitehead's observation that analyzing the obvious has produced some of man's most dramatic intellectual accomplishments.) Apparently, one of man's most primitive traits is to respond to the symbols he invents as if they are whatever it is that he invented them to symbolize. The words assume, so to speak, a life of their own and can become more important than the reality they are intended to codify. An especially interesting example of this can be found in the conventional responses to "dirty words," by, say, the U.S. Post Office, which acts as our official censor of published materials. Post Office officials rarely, if ever, object to a description of sexual activities provided that an author has used a certain set of verbal symbols. However, if the author has chosen "dirty words" to describe the same events, he may find himself in court and possibly in prison. It is not the event itself that distresses the Post Office. It is the words.

The two kinds of "semantic awareness" described above comprise the basis for what can be called "consciousness of the process of abstraction." That is, consciousness of the fact that out of a virtually infinite universe of possible things to pay attention to, we abstract only certain portions, and those portions turn out to be the ones for which we have verbal labels or categories. What we abstract, i.e., "see," and how we abstract it, or see it or think about it, is for all practical purposes inseparable from how we talk about it. This is what all of the people in the quotations appended to this chapter are saying.

A third kind of semantic awareness is an extension of the consciousness of abstracting, namely, an awareness of varying levels of abstraction. Words vary in the degree to which they correspond to verifiable referents. Some words are relatively more abstract or general, and some words relatively more concrete or specific. Related to this fact is a fourth kind of semantic awareness, which might be called the "direction of meaning." That is, with increasingly abstract or general words (i.e., those farther removed from operationally verifiable referents), the direction of meaning shifts accordingly from "outside" to "inside." With increasingly concrete or specific words (i.e., those whose referents can be more easily verified operationally), the direction of meaning shifts accordingly from "inside" to "outside."

The conventional semantic terminology for these directions of meaning are *intensional* (internal or inside) and *extensional* (external or outside). Closely bound to these directions of meaning are, of course, different kinds of meaning. The primary semantic distinction made in kinds of meaning is between *connotation* (intensional, subjective, personal meaning) and *denotation* (extensional, objective, social meaning).

Scientific language, which Korzybski used as his model of sane language, is almost exclusively extensional and denotative, or at least tries to be. The language of the mentally ill, most obviously "un-sane," is almost totally intensional and connotative This is language which does not correspond to anything "out there," and this is, in fact, how and perhaps even why the user is mentally ill. Korzybski's concern with keeping conscious "connection" or correspondence between language and verifiable referents is, for all practical purposes, paralleled by the process of psychotherapy. In this process, which is largely "just talk," the purpose is to foster closer and more accurate correspondence between the patient's language and externally verifiable meanings. As a semanticist would say, the process of psychotherapy is aimed at shifting the patient's word choices from those having highly intensional, connotative meanings to others carrying more denotative meanings. A person suffering from paranoid schizophrenia might use perfectly "correct" English in an unassailably "logical" way, but the problem with his language is that it does not correspond to anything "out there."

And this is the essential basis for the semanticist's contention that sanity is a function of the degree to which language corresponds to things externally verifiable.

A fifth kind of semantic awareness has to do with what might be called the "photographic" effects of language. We live in a universe of constant process. Everything is changing in the physical world around us. We ourselves, physically at least, are always changing. Out of this maelstrom of happenings we abstract certain bits to attend to. We snapshot these bits my naming them. Then we begin responding to the names as if they are the bits we have named, thus obscuring the effects of change. The names we use tend to "fix" that which is named, particularly if the names also carry emotional connotations. For example, physicians warn us not to keep medicine stored in our medicine cabinets much beyond the date for which they were prescribed because their chemistry—along with everything else—keeps changing. What might have been therapeutically valuable at one time may have fatal effects at another—even though its *name* remains the same. There are some semanticists who have suggested that such phrases as "national defense" and "national sovereignty" have been similarly maintained beyond the date for which they were prescribed. What might have been politically therapeutic at one time may prove politically fatal at another.

A variation on the "photographic" effect of language consists of noting how blurred the photograph is. "Blurring" occurs as a result of general class names, rendering distinctions among individual members of the class less visible. One of the most common manifestations of the lack of this kind of semantic awareness can be found in what is called "prejudice": a response to an individual is predetermined because the name of the class in which that person is included is prejudged negatively. The most obvious and ordinary remark made in cases of this kind, "They are all alike," makes the point clear.

Other forms of blurring can be found in the most ordinary, everyday statements, such as "Teenagers are irresponsible" or "Boys who wear their hair long are troublemakers" or "Bearded beatniks should be put in the Army." Another kind of blurring is oversimplification. This is commonly a statement of a problem that leaves out critical details. What characterizes most oversimplification is the attribution of single causality to complex problems. Today, for example, the tendency is to attribute to communist inspiration any political event that is found disconcerting. The ubiquitous communist is the single cause of anything untoward, from student demonstrations on the West Coast to Negro upheavals in the cities. This tendency to oversimplify has a long history, and it is easier for us to identify it in another time and place. Recognizing it here and now is not only difficult but it also requires courage.

Oversimplification, of course, has the effect of allowing action to be taken immediately, without one's enduring the burden of undergoing a process of extensional ("out there") verification. Our judicial process represents one attempt by society to minimize oversimplification by insisting upon authentic observations, the verification of facts, and the process of rigorous semantic evaluation (e.g., prosecution-defense dialogue). When oversimplification is not controlled, it produces both violence in domestic affairs and indiscriminate bombing of "enemy territory" in war. That it serves more to complicate the problem than to solve it seems (at the time at least) to be too romantic an observation to be taken seriously.

This brief list by no means includes all the kinds of awareness toward which general semantics addresses itself. But it is enough, we think, to provide a basis for intelligent inquiry into any "subject." What would a class be like if such concepts were kept at the center of all its inquiries? Below is an excerpt from a transcribed social-studies lesson. The lesson is inductive, question-centered, and, as you will see, almost entirely language-centered.

[*A discussion of the civil-rights movement is in process.*]

TEACHER: Well, then, what does "civil rights" mean?

ROD: You're joking.

TEACHER: Me?

ROD: Well, I mean, doesn't it depend on who is defining it? I don't think Stokely Carmichael and Thurmond would see it in the same way.

TEACHER: Do you mean Strom Thurmond?

ROD: Yes.

LOUIS: That may be true and all that, but what difference does it make? Thurmond or anyone else can't change the facts.

TEACHER: What facts?

LOUIS: Like if a guy wants to buy a house or eat in a store, and they won't let him. That's a fact. You can't change it.

LARRY: You can't change what?

LOUIS: The facts, f'crying out loud.

LARRY: Well, what's a fact?

LOUIS: If you don't know what a fact is, well, it's pretty bad.

TEACHER: Wait a second, Lou. What *is* a fact, according to you?

LOUIS: According to me? Well, it isn't according to me. I don't understand this "according to me" stuff about facts. A fact is what happened. Like it's a fact I'm talking to you now. That's what's happening.

TEACHER: Are you angry now?

LOUIS: Of course I'm not angry.

TEACHER: Suppose a historian were writing a history of the events of this class. Would he report that you were angry or maybe a little hostile?

LOUIS: Of course not. He'd be lying.

PHIL: No, he wouldn't. I don't know if you're angry, Lou. But if I were doing it, I'd say you were—upset. Maybe that's not the word.

TEACHER: What word would you use, Chuck?

CHUCK: Dumb.

[*Laughter.*]

LOUIS: You're a riot.

TEACHER: Madeline?

MADELINE: Seriously. Phil used the right word. Upset. Louis is definitely upset, especially with Chuck.

BOB: Maybe he is now, but he wasn't before. He was just asking some questions.

ROD: He didn't ask any questions. He told everyone what he thought.

LOUIS: I did ask questions.

TEACHER: Well, now here are some interesting problems. Lou says that a fact is what happened. How do you know what happened? Lou says you just look. Is that right, Lou?

LOUIS: Now I'm not sure. If we had a tape recorder, we'd find out if I asked any questions or not.

TEACHER: Would we find out if you were upset, say, two minutes ago?

LOUIS: Well, if you asked me, I could tell you.

TEACHER: But how can we account for the fact that others did think you were upset?

BOB: How do we know it's a fact that others thought that?

CHUCK: Oh, my god!

ROD: Look. There's a point everyone's missing. The thing about "angry" and "upset" is important. What a person *says* happened may not be what happened, but that's all your historian—any history writer—could do anyway. *Say* what happened. I might say Lou was "upset." You—he was "happy." Chuck, "dumb."

TEACHER: Are you implying that a fact is not what happened, but a statement about what happened?

ROD: I think so. I mean, who knows what happened? No one can see everything. Or hear. You just say what you think you saw.

TEACHER: Well, in that case, if we couldn't even get agreement on whether or not Lou was angry, wouldn't it be even more difficult to determine when someone's "civil rights" are being violated?

ADAM: It's hard but not impossible.

TEACHER: What do you mean?

ADAM: Well, after all, people do communicate, don't they? And history is communication.

TEACHER: History is communication?

ADAM: Yeah. I like that.

[*Laughter.*]

TEACHER: Congratulations. But what do you mean by it?

ADAM: Well, you know, if history is saying words about things, then it's communication. And if it's communication, there must be some rules to figure out how good someone is communicating. Like take the thing with Lou. Suppose someone wrote that Lou cursed. You would check it out by asking everyone, or by a tape recorder.

TEACHER: Do you remember Lou cursing?

ADAM: No.

TEACHER: I remember he said, "f'crying out loud."

LOUIS: That's not a curse—f'crying out loud.

[*Laughter.*]

ADAM: I know what you're getting at. Okay. Maybe "curse" is too vague. But suppose a guy wrote that Lou punched someone. You could check that. And everyone would agree. Most everyone, anyway. Because you [*to the teacher*] don't agree with anything.

[*Laughter.*]

TEACHER: Well, suppose you obtained agreement from everyone but me, how would you handle me?

MADELINE: If everyone agreed except you?

TEACHER: Yes.

MADELINE: I'd want to know why you didn't agree. Maybe you just want to give everyone a hard time.

TEACHER: You mean, you'd question my motives?

MADELINE: Why not? Some people want something to come out the way they want it to come out.

TEACHER: And how would we determine whose statements about something are the most reliable?

CHUCK: You could go to court.

[*Laughter.*]

No. Seriously. Like in court, there are rules about when a guy can be trusted. Like a witness, I mean. Sometimes a judge says, "Rule that statement out."
TEACHER: Are the rules in court the same as the rules for judging historical statements?
CHUCK: That's an interesting question. Are they?

Obviously, from our point of view, the most important thing going on in this lesson is that the students are *thinking* (and apparently enjoying it). But it is equally important that they are beginning to think the way historians think, that is, they are struggling with the kinds of problems that any historian must face. Although it sometimes comes as a surprise to many history teachers, almost all of these problems have to do with language and perception. (And nothing to do, incidentally, with memorizing dates.) The students in the class, therefore, are learning about language *and* history because, in fact, the two are inseparable.

In this connection, the "structure" of this particular class is worth commenting on. The students began their term's work by considering several questions, one of which was "What are some of the important changes occurring in society now?" One of their answers was "the civil-rights movement." This answer led to several other questions, such as, "What is a 'movement'?," "What is a 'civil right'?" and, as demonstrated in the lesson above, "What is a 'fact'?" and "How can you determine whose 'facts' are reliable?" Following this lesson, the teacher (at first) and the students (later) provided problem after problem in fact discrimination. For example, taking a cue from Chuck, the teacher gave the students the following problem in the language of courtrooms:

> Here is the transcript of part of the trial of Louis Conchi, accused of homicide. The District Attorney is questioning an eyewitness to the alleged murder, hoping thereby to establish Conchi's guilt. Read the transcript carefully:

DISTRICT ATTORNEY: Mr. Flood, will you tell the court precisely what you saw on the night of February 6, 1965, at approximately 11 P.M.

MR. FLOOD: Well, it was pretty simple. I was riding along in my car and I saw Conchi and Mr. Lewis fighting at the edge of the bridge.

DISTRICT ATTORNEY: Did you take any action?

MR. FLOOD: I stopped my car, got out, and ran toward the two men.

DISTRICT ATTORNEY: And?

MR. FLOOD: Well, before I reached them, this murderer pushed Mr. Lewis off the bridge.

DISTRICT ATTORNEY: Did you do or say anything?

MR. FLOOD: Well, yes. I grabbed him by the arm and swung him around.

DISTRICT ATTORNEY: Did the defendant resist?

MR. FLOOD: He sure did. He grabbed my arm and I knew from his face that he would throw me off the bridge, too.

DISTRICT ATTORNEY: Did the defendant say anything to you?

MR. FLOOD: He threatened me. "If you don't get back, there'll be trouble," he said.

DISTRICT ATTORNEY: And did you get back?

MR. FLOOD: You're darn right I did. With a crazy maniac like that—why, he'd just as soon kill two people as one.

DISTRICT ATTORNEY [*turning to Defense Attorney*]: Your witness, Mr. Denning.

[*Imagine that you are Mr. Denning, defense counsel for Mr. Conchi.*

1. At what points in the District Attorney's examination of Mr. Flood would you have raised objections?

2. On what grounds would you have objected?

3. During your cross-examination, what further questions would you ask the witness about his testimony?]

This problem was followed by others, such as a comparison of two different descriptions of the Monroe Doctrine; a comparison of several different accounts (from the newspapers) of an "election" in Vietnam; a comparison of the descriptions of the "American Revolution" in the *Encyclopaedia Britannica* and the *Encyclopedia Americana;* a comparison of the treatment of the "Nazi regime" in three different high-school text-books; comparisons of the students' own descriptions of certain events; and so on.

Through such language inquiries as these the students were able to learn something about "history." For example, that there is no such thing as "history," only histories; that there is no such thing as "objectivity," only degrees of subjectivity; that whatever you say something is, it isn't; that one's defini-tions, assumptions, and metaphors determine what "facts" one will uncover; that the world is in a constant process of change and that we can never "see" it all; that each of our senses is a censor, and so is each of our sentences. In short, the students began to learn how one *does* history, how one reads it, and how one uses it.

The idea that the study of any subject is essentially a study of language seems to be recognized everywhere except in school. A moment's reflection on what constitutes *inquiry* will reveal that practically the entire process consists of language operations. If we allow that inquiry involves question asking, defining, observing, classifying, generalizing, verifying, and theorizing, then the inseparability of language and inquiry is obvious. But of course the inquiry language of different "sub-jects" varies—and in some cases considerably. What, for ex-ample, is a "fact" in biology? Is it the same as a "fact" in mathematics? Does mathematics have any "facts"? What are the characteristics of a "historical generalization"? Are they the same as a "generalization" in chemistry? What does "law" mean in biology, linguistics, psychology, or physics? What does "theory" mean as you shift from "subject" to "subject"?

Or consider the seemingly simple word "answer." Let us examine how the languaging process is involved in producing what we call "answers." Whether we are studying a "subject," working a crossword puzzle, or dealing with daily affairs, we seem to be trying to find answers. However, we rarely distin-guish among the different kinds of answers we seek: an answer is an answer, and that's that. What happens when we fail to make distinctions? One possibility is that we can come up with an "answer" that is irrelevant: it doesn't work, or do what it is supposed to. Answers of this kind are most obvious when made by physicians or mechanics or politicians, whose answers can be seen in action. A physician's irrelevant answer to "What's wrong?" results in a treatment that usually makes the problem worse, not better. A mechanic's answer can result in a big repair bill for something that doesn't help the car to function better. A Secretary of State's "answer" can lead to needless killing and destruction.

As we have implied, one way to minimize knowing an irrelevant answer is to make distinctions among different kinds of answers. Perhaps the most useful strategy to employ is to determine what kind of system you are confronted by. System, in this context, refers to situations in which we are trying to "know" something, in which we are trying to assign meanings. A crossword puzzle may be viewed as a system (of meanings). So may geometry, history, mathematics, as well as medicine, international relations, business, and astrophysics. However, not all of these systems are alike. For example, they differ greatly in the degree to which they are "closed" and "open." A closed system is one in which the knowables are fixed. Examples of this kind of system would include any in which most of its answers are either yes or no, right or wrong, clearly and without any other possibility. Most mathematical problems are closed systems (at least as they are presented in school). There is a right answer, within the limits of the system, and any other is wrong. Some "moral" and "legal" answers are of this type. There is a right and wrong; no imagination is required. Since most of our formal training consists of learning to make *decisions* (yes-no answers in closed systems), we tend to assume that this approach is applicable to all situations. Even when we are trying to be open-minded, we are likely to say, "Let's look at both sides of the question," or "Let's hear the other side of the story." Note what happens when we talk this way: the words we use to pattern the problem force only two possibilities, and these are automatically assumed to be in opposition. Of course, if we do this with most questions, what we do in effect is to make closed systems of largely open ones. Open systems may be thought of as situations in which there are degrees of "rightness," and in which a right answer today may well be a wrong answer tomorrow. If we are not aware of whether we are working in a closed system or open one, we can consistently arrive at answers that are at best frustrating and at worst tragic.

Very few problems of any great significance can be answered if they are approached from a "closed"-system point of view. Most human problems require us to make *choices* and to find *solutions*. We mean by a "choice," the selection of one possibility from among several. This is a much more complicated and rigorous process thán making a decision. We have to include more, recognize more, consider more, and provide for more—of everything. A solution is an answer we come up with as a result of seeing about as openly as a human being can. Most scientific investigations produce solutions. Space questions, for example, are approached as an open system in which answers, frequently without any precedent, are sought. An astrophysicist is rarely frustrated when he is confronted by something he didn't expect to see. He rather expects to see all kinds of things he didn't expect to see, and he knows that what he sees at any one point in space-time may not be "true" at any future moment. Anything different from what was expected is "admitted" into the system, leading the scientist to change his perception and actions as a consequence. Both astrophysics and nuclear physics provide excellent illustrations of what we have been saying about the relationship between "knowing" and the symbol system within which human knowing happens. In both of these fields, tho knowers have had to invent all kinds of new symbols to encode the new to-be-knowns. The old symbols and symbol systems, both verbal and mathematical, simply did not "work." The language of Newtonian physics, a relatively closed system, consists of patterns, assumptions, and points of view that did not provide for the degree of simultaneous complexity that must be "seen" in order to "do" anything in astrophysics or nuclear physics. New languages had to be developed in order to open the system.

One finds a similar development in religion. In many varieties of Christianity, the orthodox were traditionally offered a series of relatively closed propositions. Some belief or action was either right or wrong, and one simply made a decision for one or the other. The emergence now of "situational ethics" presents a much more open set of problems, in which one must take into account a large number of factors. For example, on the question of the ethics of premarital sex, the closed-system religionists had a clear decision to make. Today, increasingly, ministers are suggesting that the problem is not so simple. There are these questions to be raised: Who, if anyone, will be hurt by this action? Is there a feeling of responsibility toward each other? What are the possible psychological consequences? And so on. As in the new physics, the new religion represents, essentially, a new language. As a system moves from closed to open, a new coding structure is always needed in order to permit productive thinking to occur. For example, how useful are the following terms: original sin, miracle, god-fearing, redemption, salvation, etc.? Some theologians are even suggesting that the word "god" itself is no longer useful in helping people to make the choices and find the solutions that the conditions of their lives require.

The same situation is found in politics. "My country right or wrong" may have been adequate as a guiding principle in a simpler world. But the Nuremberg Trials changed that. Eichmann's decision to do what his government asked him to do was universally condemned, and now the rest of us are faced with complex choices. What are the "best" meanings of patriotism, loyalty, national interest, etc.? Do we require a new language of citizenship? Apparently, yes, because citizenship is no longer a closed system of clear obligations. We most certainly require a new language of war. In an earlier time, a nation either won or lost. There was only one question to ask: How can we win? Today, it is not so simple. We must ask, "What are the consequences of 'winning'?" "What would constitute 'winning'?" "Can we gain advantages by 'losing'?" And so on. It goes without saying that the relentless series of disastrous decisions in Vietnam have been made by men who are accustomed to using a language that is no longer adequate to represent the reality they must deal with.

The usual method of evaluating students in school provides still another example of how important it is to make distinctions between the kinds of systems you are confronted with, and among the kinds of answers that can be produced. In most cases, decisions are made about the performance of children. For example, the question is asked, "Can he do math or can't he?" Of course, if the "answer" is no, we can be sure that the child will *become* that answer. If, instead, a choice were to be made about him, the questions (plural) would be, "What does he know about math?" "What might he learn?" etc. If a solution is sought, the questions are something like "Why is he having trouble learning math?" "How can we minimize or eliminate the causes of the trouble?" etc. Naturally, if a solution is sought, the student's chances for improvement are best.

We want to stress at this point that we are not especially committed to our particular terminology (open-closed; decision-choice-solution). Perhaps you can think of more useful terms. Our intention is to help make visible a strategy of inquiry. What this means in the context of the new education is this: in the world in which we live, there are fewer and fewer closed systems that have any relevance either to knowledge or to life. Our students will need the most frequent opportunities to think about problems in an open way; that is, to make choices and to find solutions. Closed problems simply leave out too much to produce a viable answer to any question except one that is so abstract that the answer doesn't make any difference to human beings as they go about the business of trying to cope with an ever-changing environment. Look back at the questions we posed in Chapter V. You will notice that all of them require "open system" inquiries. It would be entirely possible, of course, to create a curriculum based on an analysis of systems. Such a curriculum could coexist with or develop from a questions curriculum, and it would provide students with a continuous experience in studying the effects of language, particularly in regard to how language operates to "close" or "open" the mind. One possible pattern of questions that might be used is as follows:

These questions, with variations and modifications, may be used as the basis for examining any system (e.g., the home, the government, mathematics, historical description, war, marriage, astrophysics, the school, suburbia, the draft, etc.).

What are the purposes of the system?
What roles are people assigned?
What rules must be followed?
What rights and restrictions are given and imposed?
What are some of its critical, underlying assumptions?
What are its key words?
To what extent do the problems of the system require decisions? choices? solutions?
To what extent is the system changing?
What are the mechanisms for change within the system?
To what extent is the language of the system obsolete?
What are the critical, nonverbal symbols of the system?
To what extent are these changing?
What is the actual effect of the system on people?
To what extent is this different from the ostensible purpose of the system?
Are there alternatives to the system?
Can we do without it?
How is the system related to other systems of knowing and behaving?

The purpose of all this, we need hardly say, is to make our students into open systems. People make themselves, or are made, "closed" systems for many reasons, most frequently because they are unaware of the extent to which they are languaging systems, and being unaware, they lock themselves into predetermined decisions by limiting their language resources. A person who is prejudiced against Negroes, for example, cannot "see" a Negro; he can only see "niggers" and decide that they are whatever his closed system predetermines them to be. He acts toward them as if they are what his system makes them. The same process is operating on a man who has predetermined with the aid of a limited, unconsciously used vocabulary what "America" is, or a poem, or a communist, or history, or mathematics. We *act* on the basis of what we "see." If we "see things" one way, we act accordingly. If we see them in another, we act differently. The ability to learn turns out to be a function of the extent to which one is capable of perception change. If a student goes through four years of school and comes out "seeing" things in the way he did when he started, he will act the same. Which means he learned nothing. If he does not act the same, it means he changed his way of talking. It's as complicated as that. And the new education requires that we face the problem. Thus, the basic language concepts which undergird the study of any question, problem, or system within a new-education curriculum would be the following:

Questions are instruments of perception.

The nature of a question (its form and assumptions) determines the nature of its answer.

Definitions and metaphors are instruments for thinking and have no authority beyond the context in which they are used.

Observing is a function of the symbol systems the observer has available to him. The more limited the symbol systems, in number and kind, the less one is able to "see."

A symbol system is, in effect, a point of view. The more ways of talking one is capable of, the more choices one can make and solutions one can invent.

Meaning is in people. Without people there are no meanings.

The more meanings one has in his experience, the more new meanings he can generate or acquire.

The level of abstraction at which one uses language in any context is an index of the extent to which one is "in touch" with reality. The higher the level, the less is the contact with reality.

Facts are statements about the world as perceived by human

beings. They are, therefore, as tentative as all human judgments.

The rules for judging the reliability and value of human perception are, themselves, language systems and have applicability only within a given context.

Because the process of knowing is inseparable from "languaging," in the new education, language (i.e., all forms of symbolic codification) is regarded as the mediator of all human perception and is used as a unifying and continuing focus of all student inquiry. Below are appended a number of quotations on this point from a wide range of authors. Since this attitude toward language is crucial to the whole thesis of this book, the quotations will support and expand the matter considerably.

MIRANDA:

Abhorred slave,
Which any print of goodness will not take,
Being capable of all ill!   I pitied thee,
Took pains to make thee speak, taught thee each hour
One thing or other: when thou didst not, savage,
Know thine own meaning, but wouldst gabble like
A thing most brutish, I endow'd thy purposes
With words that made them known.   But thy vile race,
Though thou didst learn, had that in't which good natures
Could not abide to be with; therefore wast thou
Deservedly confin'd into this rock,
Who hadst deserv'd more than a prison.

CALIBAN:

You taught me language; and my profit on't
Is, I know how to curse.   The red plague rid you
For learning me your language!

—SHAKESPEARE, *The Tempest*

The only justification for our concepts and systems of concepts is that they serve to represent the complex of our experiences; beyond this they have no legitimacy. I am convinced that the philosophers have had a harmful effect upon the progress of scientific thinking in removing certain fundamental concepts from the domain of empiricism, where they are under our control, to the intangible heights of the *a priori*.

—A. EINSTEIN, *Relativity*

The abuse of language occurs when its metaphorical nature is hidden, if the representation is *identified* with the thing represented. Therefore the linguistically hygienic use of metaphor depends on the full recognition of its limitations, that is, on critical consciousness of the generalizations, analogies, and abstractions involved.—A. RAPOPORT, *Operational Philosophy*

Since the concepts people live by are derived only from perceptions and from language and since the perceptions are received and interpreted only in light of earlier concepts, man comes pretty close to living in a house that language built. —RUSSELL F. W. SMITH, "Linguistics in Theory and in Practice," *ETC.*, Autumn 1952

The woof and warp of all thought and all research is symbols, and the life of thought and science is the life inherent in symbols; so that it is wrong to say that a good language is *important* to good thought, merely; for it is of the essence of it.

—C. S. PEIRCE, *Syllabus of Certain Topics of Logic*

Naming selects, discriminates, identifies, locates, orders, arranges, systematizes. Such activities as these are attributed to "thought" by older forms of expression, but they are much more properly attributed to language when language is seen as the living behavior of men.

—J. DEWEY and A. F. BENTLEY, *Knowing and the Known*

Language . . . does not permit the consideration of all aspects of behavior at once. An individual who wishes to speak or write about an event must use language which by necessity refers to some selected aspect of that event. A listener is capable of understanding the event in its entirety only after having studied not one but a great many selected aspects. Because this procedure is very time-consuming and renders written reports rather bulky, shortcuts are frequently taken and consequently many details are omitted. When fewer words are used and a lesser number of aspects are treated, the listener is inclined to pay too much attention to what is mentioned and disregard that which is omitted. This peculiarity of language and the resulting difficulties in the description of behavior have brought about certain verbal classifications which are not based upon the characteristics of pathology but rather upon those of the human reporter and the language he uses.

—J. RUESCH, *Disturbed Communication*

It is alarming to realize how much of traditional philosophy is merely the solemn, stately nonsense of obedience to grammatical protocol, or imprisonment in self-instituted denotation and connotation. All scientists examine their instruments to test for experimental error—but traditional philosophers never did examine their instrument, language! This has been done only in modern times, by the new analytic rather than the old synthetic kind of philosophy, and this shakes many semantic absolutists to the very roots of their being. Freud and the anthropologist further quietly bid us to examine that most ubiquitous of research instruments, ourselves—while our intellectual Brahmins screech bloody murder.

. . . The sorry fact is that our unconscious linguistic habits shape our religions and our philosophies, imprison our scientific statements about the world, are of the essence of the conflict of postulated culture with postulated culture, are involved with our wars and other human misunderstandings, and are a part even of our dreaming, our errors, and our neuroses.—W. LABARRE, *The Human Animal*

Even on the verbal level, where they are most at home, educators have done a good deal less than they might reasonably have been expected to do in explaining to young people the nature, the limitations, the huge potentialities for evil as well as for good, of that greatest of all human inventions, language. Children should be taught that words are indispensable but also can be fatal—the only begetters of all civilization, all science, all consistency of high purpose, all angelic goodness, and the only begetters at the same time of all superstition, all collective madness and stupidity, all worse-than-bestial diabolism, all the dismal historical succession of crimes in the name of God, King, Nation, Party, Dogma. Never before, thanks to the techniques of mass communication, have so many listeners been so completely at the mercy of so few speakers. Never

have misused words—those hideously efficient tools of all ty-
rants, warmongers, persecutors, and heresy-hunters—been so
widely and so disastrously influential as they are today. Generals, clergymen, advertisers, and all the rulers of totalitarian
states—all have good reason for disliking the idea of universal
education in the rational use of language. To the military,
clerical, propagandist, and authoritarian mind such training
seems (and rightly seems) profoundly subversive. To those
who think that liberty is a good thing, and who hope that
it may some day become possible for more people to realize
more of their desirable potentialities in a society fit for free,
fully human individuals to live in, a thorough education in
the nature of language, in its uses and abuses, seems indispensable. Whether in fact the mounting pressures of over-
population and overorganization in a world still enthusiastically
dedicated to nationalistic idolatory will permit this kind of
subversive linguistic education to be adopted by even the
more democratic nations remains to be seen.

—A. HUXLEY, "Education on the Nonverbal Level,"
Daedalus, Spring 1962

Every language is a special way of looking at the world and
interpreting experience. . . . One sees and hears what the
grammatical system of one's language has made one sensitive
to, has trained one to look for in experience. This bias is insidious because everyone is so unconscious of his native language as a system.—C. KLUCKHOHN, Mirror for Man

Einstein pointed out that the statement "Two events some
distance apart occur simultaneously" cannot be used to derive
any observable fact. Here was the impetus to a new philosophy
whose chief preoccupation has been with the meaning of language. Since all knowledge must be set forth in language, it
is the meaning we give to language which confers upon knowledge its weight and ambiguity. . . . What is curious is the
fact that we look so seldom at the phenomenon of language,
whose role in the world of affairs has no parallel.

—W. S. BECK, M.D., Modern Science and the Nature of Life

We dissect nature along lines laid down by our native language. The categories and types that we isolate from the world
of phenomena we do not find there because they stare every

observer in the face; on the contrary, the world is presented in a kaleidoscopic flux of impressions which has to be organized by our minds—and this means largely by the linguistic system in our minds. We cut nature up, organize it into concepts, and ascribe significance as we do largely because we are parties to an agreement to organize it in this way—an agreement that holds throughout our speech community and is codified in the patterns of our language.

—B. L. WHORF, *Language, Thought, and Reality*
ed. by J. B. Carroll

The worker in the laboratory does not merely report and expound by the aid of analogy; that is how he thinks, also. The atom was once a hard little round particle, or later one with hooks on it. Recently it was a solar system. The classical dispute of physics about the nature of light was really asking, Is light like a shower of pebbles, or like ripples in a bathtub? The ultimate answer, Both, was one that was hard to accept. Why? Because it fitted into no preexisting conceptions; waves are waves, and pebbles are pebbles—there is nothing in common experience that has the properties of both.

—D. O. HEBB, *The Organization of Behavior*

If a conceptual distinction is to be made . . . the machinery for making it ought to show itself in language. If a distinction cannot be made in language it cannot be made conceptually.

—N. R. HANSON, *Patterns of Discovery*

When the mind is thinking, it is talking to itself.—PLATO

Language, as such, is man's primary vehicle for thinking. Brains think with words. It is not mere verbal play to say that we cannot think without speaking, or speak without thinking. Most men suffer acute mental discomfort until the urge to express an idea, to define, to reason, to interpret has been formulated in words or in formulae, diagrams, equations or other symbolic devices which involve words. Without properly ordered specific words, thought is vague and misty, seen dimly through the depth of "feeling" and "intuition."

—J. O. HERTZLER, *A Sociology of Language*

Understanding is nothing else than conception caused by speech.—T. HOBBES, *Leviathan*

Human beings do not live in the objective world alone, nor alone in the world of social activity as ordinarily understood, but are very much at the mercy of the particular language which has become the medium of expression for their society. It is quite an illusion to imagine that one adjusts to reality essentially without the use of language and that language is merely an incidental means of solving specific problems of communication and reflection. The fact of the matter is that the "real world" is to a large extent unconsciously built up on the language habits of the group.

—E. SAPIR, *Culture, Language, and Personality*

Knowledge . . . has greater connexion with words than is commonly suspected.

—J. LOCKE, *Essay Concerning Human Understanding*

The purpose of Newspeak was not only to provide a medium of expression for the world-view and mental habits proper to the devotees of Ingsoc, but to make all other modes of thought impossible.—G. ORWELL, *1984*

There is a basic scheme of classification *built into* our commor speech and language. This built-in classification system directs us so that we observe the things we can readily classify with the names we know, while we tend strongly to overlook or disregard everything else. We see with our categories.

—W. JOHNSON, *Verbal Man*

Before the intellectual work of conceiving and understanding of phenomena can set in, the work of *naming* must have preceded it, and have reached a certain point of elaboration. For it is this process which transforms the world of sense impression, which animals also possess, into a mental world, a world of ideas and meanings. All theoretical cognition takes its departure from a world already preformed by language; the scientist, the historian, even the philosopher, lives with his objects only as language presents them to him. This immediate dependence is harder to realize than anything that the mind creates mediately, by conscious thought processes.

—E. CASSIRER, *Language and Myth*

The world is much, much greater than our way of words with it. As J. B. S. Haldane—a great scientist—once said: "The universe is not only stranger than we suppose; it is stranger than we *can* suppose."

We find the discoveries of modern science, or the utterances of modern writing, strange, but much of this strangeness is due to our provincialism concerning language—especially our own language. Insofar as we Westerners conceive of the universe as a collection of simple "things" distinct in nature, yet taking part in "actions," we are certainly doing that universe an injustice.—M. GIRSDANSKY, *The Adventure of Language*

Language is not only the medium, by which all our thoughts, feelings, emotions, and ideas are obtained from and communicated to others, but language is the instrument by which the mind itself acts. This is so true, that we think in words, we cannot reason or reflect, except by words. They are the very material on which the mind works, and the implements with which it works.

    —JUDGE L. SHAW (to whom Melville dedicated *Typee;* see *Herman Melville: Cycle and Epicycle* by Elinor Melville Metcalf)

Words play their familiar tricks even with the thinking of the scientist, who may forget that in his necessary use of word symbols for his thinking and communication (space, time, IQ, attitude, etc.) he is employing abstractions which he cannot, as a scientist, implicitly or unconsciously assume as real in investigation. It is only to the extent that the investigator is aware of his own transformation of adjectival or adverbial relationships into noun qualities that he maintains the possibility of discovering new conditional relationships except for which a phenomenon would not exist.

    —F. P. KILPATRICK, *Explorations in Transactional Psychology*

The denial that language is of the essence of thought, is not the assertion that thought is possible apart from the other activities coordinated with it. Such activities may be termed the expression of thought. When these activities satisfy certain conditions, they are termed a language.

    —A. N. WHITEHEAD, *Modes of Thought*

Diagnosis is changing because we are changing our concepts of illness and disease. . . . But it is very difficult to rid our thinking and our language of the old entity concept of illness. We often speak in figurative terms of "fighting the disease," "facing it," of having a cancer, of suffering from arthritis, or of being afflicted with high blood pressure. This argot reflects the tendency to go on thinking of all diseases as a thing, a horrid, hateful, alien thing which invades the organism. . . .

But one truth which has to be learned, and re-learned, and re-learned again, because we continually forget it, is that two apparently opposite things can be true. It is sometimes true that disease is an invasion; in other instances it is just as true that disease is not an invasion.

. . . Illness is in part what the world has done to a victim, but in a larger part it is what the victim has done with his world, and with himself. . . .

What we are objecting to is the inference so easily drawn that the diagnostic labels in common use to describe psychiatric conditions are as definite and constant as those of Tay-Sachs disease. . . . Diagnostic name-calling may be damning. . . . The very word "cancer" is said to kill some patients who would not have succumbed (so quickly) to the malignancy from which they suffer. . . . We disparage labelling of all kinds in psychiatry insofar as these labels apply to supposed diseases or conditions of specific etiological determination. We deplore the tendency of psychiatry to retain its old pejorative name-calling functions. Patients who consult us because of their suffering and their distress and their disability have every right to resent being plastered with a damning index tab. Our function is to help these people, not to further afflict them.

—KARL MENNINGER, *The Vital Balance*

The reason why Taoism and Zen present, at first sight, such a puzzle to the Western mind is that we have taken a restricted view of human knowledge. For us, almost all knowledge is what a Taoist would call conventional knowledge, because we do not feel that we really know anything unless we can represent it to ourselves in words, or in some other system of conventional signs such as the notations of mathematics and music. Such knowledge is called conventional because it is a matter of social agreement as to the codes of communication. Just as people speaking the same language have tacit agreements as to what words shall stand for what things, so the members

of every society and every culture are united by bonds of communication resting upon all kinds of agreement as to the classification and valuation of actions and things.

Thus the task of education is to make children fit to live in
a society by persuading them to learn and accept its codes—
the rules and conventions of communication whereby the
society holds itself together. There is first the spoken language.
The child is taught to accept "tree" and not "boojum" as the
agreed sign for that (pointing to the object). We have no
difficulty in understanding that the word "tree" is a matter of
convention. What is much less obvious is that convention also
governs the delineation of the thing to which the word is
assigned. For the child has to be taught not only what words
are to stand for what things, but also the way in which his
culture has tacitly agreed to divide things from each other, to
mark out the boundaries within our daily experience. Thus,
scientific convention decides whether an eel shall be a fish or
a snake, and grammatical convention determines what experiences shall be called objects and what shall be called events
or actions. How arbitrary such conventions may be can be seen
from the question, "What happens to my fist (noun-object)
when I open my hand?" The object miraculously vanishes because an action was disguised by a part of speech usually
asigned to a thing! In English the differences between things
and actions are clearly, if not always logically, distinguished
but a great number of Chinese words do duty for both nouns
and verbs—so that one who thinks in Chinese has little difficulty in seeing that objects are also events, that our world is a
collection of processes rather than entities.

—ALAN WATTS, *The Way of Zen*

Words are a special class of symbols. In earliest life, verbaliza-
tion serves a strictly autistic, primary-process function. The
individual derives instinctual pleasure purely from perception
of sound and sensation. Words first enter the psychic life
rooted in association to body parts, products, and needs. They
gradually become attached to concrete objects outside the self,
and later represent more abstract concepts of objects. As language develops through the use of conventionalized symbols
shared by others, early connections with body image and functions are repressed, and the shared associations between word

symbol and the objects or ideas symbolized remain conscious. Word symbolization makes possible a large part of interpersonal communication and of conceptualization, forming the basis of secondary-process thinking.

In states of regression, primary-process thought progressively resumes domination of language through loss of consensually validated symbolization. Shared meanings for words are replaced by strictly personal meanings, frequently closely related to body image and function. Ability to form abstractions gives way to concretization in which a word denotes a very specific object and loses its broader connotation. Differentiation between word symbol and the object represented recedes until a complete equation occurs between them, and the word for an object can generate the same affect as the object itself. Words may become interchangeable substitutes for each other and for the objects symbolized.

—BEULAH PARKER, M.D., *My Language Is Me*

The development of language reflects back upon thought; for with language thoughts may become organized, new thoughts evolved. Self-awareness and the sense of social responsibility have arisen as a result of organized thoughts. Systems of ethics and law have been built up. Man has become self-conscious, responsible, a social creature.

—C. CHERRY, *On Human Communication*

How does language promote thinking? Very much as one might expect; since there are two main aspects to language, meanings expressed in vocabulary and relationships in grammar and rhetoric, language promotes thinking by both means. Let us take the first. Brains think with words. Perhaps they need not. Supposedly if we had no words, we should still be able to think. But it is the nature of human brains that they think so much better with words than with any other medium —with mental pictures, for instance—that, words being available, we learn to think with them, and rely upon them so much that for practical purposes most people think only about things for which they have words and can think only in the directions for which they have words.—C. LAIRD, *The Miracle of Language*

Language is far more than a means for exchanging information and ideas or an outlet for pent-up emotions: it reveals and expresses a special way of looking at the world and interpreting experience. Every language conceals within its structure a vast array of unconscious assumptions about life and the universe, all that you take for granted and everything that seems to make common sense—the long forgotten history of thought itself, still coercing the living to think along the old established ways. Speech itself imprisons us, although in different ways, and each kind expresses a different view. What is sense to you may be nonsense to another, or the other way round. Each sees but a part, yet it is our supernal purpose to see the whole, and each human race needs to see through the eyes of another.

You cannot, for instance, get a straight "yes or no" answer from a Chinese unless he is thinking and speaking in your language and not his own, for Chinese has no equivalents for such words or for their meanings, for Chinese thinking does not run to "is it this or was it that" but to "how is it or in what way."—N. J. BERRILL, *Man's Emerging Mind*

"When *I* use a word," Humpty Dumpty said, in a rather scornful tone, "it means just what I choose it to mean—neither more nor less."

"The question is," said Alice, "whether you *can* make words mean so many different things."

"The question is," said Humpty Dumpty, "which is to be master—that's all."—LEWIS CARROLL, *Through the Looking-Glass*

VIII. New Teachers

IF WHAT YOU HAVE READ so far has made sense to you, you have probably anticipated us by asking, "Where do we get the new teachers necessary to translate the new education into action?"

Obviously, it will be very difficult to get many of them from the old education. Most of these have a commitment to existing metaphors, procedures, and goals that would preclude their accepting a "new education." Below is an article that appeared in *The New York Times*, August 1, 1967. We reproduce it in its entirety because it includes several of the reasons that so many people now teaching would be unable to adapt to new conditions.

TEACHERS SCORED BY YOUTH PANEL

*Lack of Communication Is
Called Crux of Problem
by 10 Teen-Agers*

VIEWS ARE CHALLENGED

Some of the 150 Instructors
in Audience Walk Out
in Heated Exchange

Ten teen-agers told a group of teachers yesterday that going to some schools was "worse than no education at all," because of racial discrimination, narcotics and other classroom problems.

"You aren't going to like this," 15-year-old Cynthia Smith said, as she began to describe the "behave yourself or get out" method of discipline in her junior high school. About 150 teachers were listening in the auditorium of the Sarah J. Hale High School in Brooklyn.

Some of the teachers challenged the teen-agers' complaints. Several young women, murmuring "I can't take this any longer," left. Shortly after Deputy Mayor Timothy W. Costello appeared at the session, a school official asked Fran Defren, a neighborhood poverty worker, to change the topic "so that this won't disintegrate into a shouting match."

The teen-agers, many of them high school dropouts who now work for the South Brooklyn Community Progress Center, the local arm of the poverty program, had asked Board of Education officials to arrange the meeting. They contended that the cause of most classroom problems was an "almost total" lack of communication between teen-agers and adults.

More Talking Urged

"The teachers don't want to communicate with us," 18-year-old Louis Gelomino said. "But they should. A long talk is much more effective than just taking a failing student aside and saying, 'You have two 65's and three 40's, and it looks bad for you.'"

Dave Hamilton, 15, complained that the only time he heard his principal's voice was over his school's loud speaker system.

"The principal goes into his office every morning and says into the microphone, 'Junior High School 51 is the best'," Dave said, "and he knows that's a lie."

Some of the teachers, however, blamed the youths for not trying hard enough to communicate. "Every time I try to talk to a student he gives me the brush off," a young Puerto Rican teacher said.

"You have to keep searching in South Brooklyn," Louis Gelomino answered. "You'll find a few responsive ones. This area may be physically repugnant to you, but a lot of the people are beautiful."

"I think a lot of the trouble comes from a lack of love between students and teachers," 19-year-old Georg McLaughlin added.

"It's not my job to love my pupils—it's my job to teach them," a teacher shouted back.

Discrimination Charged

The panel—made up of Negro, Puerto Rican and white teenagers—cited racial discrimination as another problem. Cynthia Smith told the teachers, about 95 per cent of whom are white, that only two teachers in Junior High School 10 were Negro.

"There are four," came a voice from the audience.

Jerrold Glassman, a former principal at the school, said that three of about 70 teachers there are Negro. The school will be replaced by Intermediate School 88 this fall.

Joe Castagna, 18, complained about methods of discipline. "I had a chemistry teacher at John Jay High School who made unruly kids sit in the back of the room and read comic books. If you read comic books until the end of the term, you passed," he said.

Isador Auerbach, principal of John Jay until last September, when asked about the chemistry teacher, said, "I'm sure nothing like that has ever gone on."

Later, over turkey sandwiches and pickles in the school lunchroom, many teachers conceded they knew their students' problems, but were unable to help them.

"Many students get angry, but when it happens in the classroom, there's no place to talk," said Alaine Mitchell, a teacher at Junior High School 142. Other teachers complained that time they wanted to spend with students was taken up with "needless" paper work.

A middle-aged teacher, who declined to give her name, commented that parochial schools were "above" having problems.

"In the parochial schools," she said, "if we have a problem child, we threaten him with public school. They shape up."

A few paragraphs from the article require special attention. For example, you noted, we are sure, that some of the teachers walked out of the meeting. You noted, too, that the subject had to be changed before it turned into "a shouting match." And what was the subject? Communication, and how to facilitate it between students and teachers. We think it safe to assume that the teachers who left because they couldn't "take this any longer" are useless in the new education. Remember: in order for a perception to change one must be frustrated in one's actions or change one's purpose. Remember, too, that no one can force anyone else to change his perception. It might take a lifetime for anyone to create the conditions that would permit these teachers to modify their perceptions. This is especially true for the teacher who, in response to a student's plea for love, shouted back, "It's not my job to love my pupils—it's my job to teach them." And how, one wonders, does he think you "teach them"? There are other teachers referred to in the article whose perceptions are apparently not so far removed from those required by the new education. We are referring to the group who, at lunch, conceded they knew their students' problems, but were unable to help them. These teachers have satisfied one of the basic conditions of perception change—a recognition of frustration resulting from their assumptions. Perhaps there is some hope there, but it is very hard to tell. Why, one asks, if these teachers *know* their students' problems can they not help them? Perhaps because they do not know their students' problems. Or perhaps because they accept as an unalterable "given" the structure of the school and cannot imagine how the students' problems can be resolved within that structure. In any event, it is clear to us that the major source of teachers for the new education will have to come from the institutions that are now training prospective teachers. Accordingly, most of this chapter will deal with what might be done in teacher training in order to produce human beings who could function in the new education. But before we turn to that, we want to make, as promised much earlier, several bizarre proposals that are designed to change the perceptions of teachers now functioning in the schools. We know from the available research that sometimes perceptions can be changed if the point of view of the perceiver is shifted. Perception change has even been known to occur when a different point of view has been *forced* on a perceiver. That is, when the perceiver is put into an environment that makes it difficult, if not impossible, for him to function with his old assumptions. In these circumstances change does not happen automatically, or often, but it does happen enough times to warrant an effort. And so we will now put before you a list of proposals that attempt to change radically the nature of the existing school environment. Most of them will strike you as thoroughly impractical but only because you will have forgotten for the moment that the present system is among the most impractical imaginable, if the facilitation of learning is your aim. There is yet another reaction you might have to our proposals. You might concede that they are "impractical" and yet feel that each one contains an idea or two that might be translated into "practical" form. If you do, we will be delighted. But as for us, none of our proposals seems impractical or bizarre. They seem, in fact, quite conservative, given the enormity of the problem they are intended to resolve. As you read them, imagine that you are a member of a board of education, or a principal, or supervisor, or some such person who might have the wish and power to lay the groundwork for a new education.

1. *Declare a five-year moratorium on the use of all textbooks.*

Since with two or three exceptions all texts are not only boring but based on the assumption that knowledge exists prior to, independent of, and altogether outside of the learner, they are either worthless or harmful. If it is impossible to function without textbooks, provide every student with a notebook filled with blank pages, and have him compose his own text.

2. *Have "English" teachers "teach" Math, Math teachers*

English, Social Studies teachers Science, Science teachers Art, and so on.

One of the largest obstacles to the establishment of a sound learning environment is the desire of teachers to get something they think they know into the heads of people who don't know it. An English teacher teaching Math would hardly be in a position to fulfill this desire. Even more important, he would be forced to perceive the "subject" as a learner, not a teacher. If this suggestion is too impractical, try numbers 3 and 4.

3. Transfer all the elementary-school teachers to high school and vice versa.

4. Require every teacher who thinks he knows his "subject" well to write a book on it.

In this way, he will be relieved of the necessity of inflicting *his* knowledge on other people, particularly his students.

5. Dissolve all "subjects," "courses," and especially "course requirements."

This proposal, all by itself, would wreck every existing educational bureaucracy. The result would be to deprive teachers of the excuses presently given for their failures and to free them to concentrate on their learners.

6. Limit each teacher to three declarative sentences per class, and 15 interrogatives.

Every sentence above the limit would be subject to a 25-cent fine. The students can do the counting and the collecting.

7. Prohibit teachers from asking any questions they already know the answers to.

This proposal would not only force teachers to perceive learning from the learner's perspective, it would help them to learn how to ask questions that produce knowledge.

8. Declare a moratorium on all tests and grades.

This would remove from the hands of teachers their major weapons of coercion and would eliminate two of the major obstacles to their students' learning anything significant.

9. Require all teachers to undergo some form of psychotherapy as part of their in-service training.

This need not be psychoanalysis; some form of group therapy or psychological counseling will do. Its purpose: to give teachers an opportunity to gain insight into themselves, particularly into the reasons they are teachers.

10. *Classify teachers according to their ability and make the lists public.*

There would be a "smart" group (the Bluebirds), an "average" group (the Robins), and a "dumb" group (the Sandpipers). The lists would be published each year in the community paper. The I.Q. and reading scores of teachers would also be published, as well as the list of those who are "advantaged" and "disadvantaged" by virtue of what they know in relation to what their students know.

11. *Require all teachers to take a test prepared by students on what the students know.*

Only if a teacher passes this test should he be permitted to "teach." This test could be used for "grouping" the teachers as in number 10 above.

12. *Make every class an elective and withhold a teacher's monthly check if his students do not show any interest in going to next month's classes.*

This proposal would simply put the teacher on a par with other professionals, e.g., doctors, dentists, lawyers, etc. No one forces you to go to a particular doctor unless you are a "clinic case." In that instance, you must take what you are given. Our present system makes a "clinic case" of every student. Bureaucrats decide who shall govern your education. In this proposal, we are restoring the American philosophy: no clients, no money; lots of clients, lots of money.

13. *Require every teacher to take a one-year leave of absence every fourth year to work in some "field" other than education.*

Such an experience can be taken as evidence, albeit shaky, that the teacher has been in contact with reality at some point in his life. Recommended occupations: bartender, cab driver, garment worker, waiter. One of the common sources of difficulty with teachers can be found in the fact that most of them simply move from one side of the desk (as students) to the other side (as "teachers") and they have not had much contact with the way things are outside of school rooms.

14. Require each teacher to provide some sort of evidence that he or she has had a loving relationship with at least one other human being.

If the teacher can get someone to say, "I love her (or him)," she should be retained. If she can get two people to say it, she should get a raise. Spouses need not be excluded from testifying.

15. Require that all the graffiti accumulated in the school toilets be reproduced on large paper and be hung in the school halls.

Graffiti that concern teachers and administrators should be chiseled into the stone at the front entrance of the school.

16. There should be a general prohibition against the use of the following words and phrases: teach, syllabus, covering ground, I.Q., makeup, test, disadvantaged, gifted, accelerated, enhancement, course, grade, score, human nature, dumb, college material, and administrative necessity.

Before proceeding to our next series of recommendations, we want to say a further word about the seriousness of the foregoing proposals. Consider, for example, proposals 14 and 15, which some people might regard as facetious, if not flippant. Proposal 14 would require a teacher to present evidence of his having had a loving relationship with another person. Silly, isn't it? What kinds of evidence must teachers presently offer to qualify for their jobs? A list of "courses." Which of these requirements strikes you as more bizarre? From the student's point of view, which requirement would seem more practical? Bear in mind that it is a very difficult thing for one person to learn anything significant from another. Bear in mind, too, that it is probably not possible for such learning to occur unless there is something resembling a loving relationship between "teacher" and learner. Then ask yourself if you can think of anything sillier than asking an applicant for a teaching job if he has taken a course in Victorian literature?

Proposal 15 concerns making the school's graffiti public in the manner in which various slogans and mottos now adorn school halls and facades. Look back at the article from *The Times*, and you will find in it a student's remark about what the principal says into the public-address system each morning. The student is obviously disgusted at the fact that the principal is lying. It is astonishing that so many people do not recognize the extent to which hypocrisy and drivel poison the whole atmosphere of school. And where will you find more concentrated hypocrisy and drivel than on the walls of classrooms, and in the halls, and on the facades of school buildings? To replace these with intimately felt observations would be neither tasteless nor eccentric. Unless, of course, your sense of propriety includes attempting to deceive the young.

Finally, we want to say that, in spite of our belief that it is unreasonable to expect the current crop of teachers to change sufficiently to permit an educational revolution to occur, it is sometimes surprising to discover how wrong we can be. There *are* teachers—some of whom have been at it for ten or 15 years —who know how desperately change is needed, and who are more than willing to be agents of such change. Such people cannot be dismissed, and, in fact, we spend a considerable amount of our time trying to locate them and lend them support. But the teachers of the future must bring this revolution off or it will not happen. Therefore, we would like to present some "conventional" proposals for the training of college students who wish to become teachers. Our proposals are intended to make possible important changes without immediately abolishing the current structure of teacher-training institutions.

Following the "medium is the message" or "you learn what you do" theme, it is obvious that teacher education must have prospective teachers *do* as students what they as teachers must help their students, in turn, to do. How might such a teacher-education program operate? In general, something like this: It would shift the prospective teacher into the role of the inventor of viable new teaching strategies. It would confront him with problems specifically intended to evoke from him questions about what he's doing, why he's doing it, what it's supposed to be good for, and how he can tell.

Such a program would affect every aspect of the existing structure of teacher training. But here we want to limit ourselves to describing a "course" which we have "taught" and which we think may serve as a model for a revolution in teacher training. What we are trying to show is how it is possible, *given the egg crate we have been put in,* to begin to make the new education possible. Our method will be, simply, to describe what we have been doing for over ten years.

The "course" may be described as a "general methods course," which is the bane of all education students and which is held in the greatest contempt by everyone in the school from the custodian to the president. The students in it are all planning to teach in high school, and they have all specialized in the usual "subject-matter areas." Our classes, then, consist of students who have "majored" in English, mathematics, science, history, foreign languages, physical education, art, music, home economics, speech, and so on. They usually feel that they have nothing in common, and they find it difficult—almost impossible —to think about their prospective students, so formidable is their concern for their "subject." One of the things this means is that they have never thought of asking—up to this point— "Why the hell should anybody be 'taught' my subject?" When this question does come up, they tend to respond with stereotypic utterances that seem to have the effect of keeping them from thinking about the question and its significance. Most of their responses, while stated differently, merely amount to "It's required" for one thing or another: for graduation, for a regents diploma, for college entrance, etc. The answer implicitly assumes that a bureaucratically imposed reason is adequate as justification. Seldom, if ever, do the responses relate to anything outside of the school's conventional parameters. "Art," "music," "phys ed.," and "home ec." "majors" sometimes manage to make reference to something about the student and his life outside the school, but not always, or even usually, so constraining is school talk about school stuff.

In any event, we have tried to disconnect these prospective teachers from their dead rhetoric by "simply" providing them with the freedom—and then the responsibility—to invent what they would construe to be the best secondary-school experience for students in the nuclear space age. We usually urge them to consider naming this venture "Quo Vadimus High School."

The trouble starts almost immediately.

It starts almost immediately because the students have been victims—in this case for almost *16 years*—of the kind of schooling we have described earlier as producing intellectual paraplegics. The college students we are now talking about are the ones who were most "successful" in conventional school terms. That is, they are the ones who learned best what they were required to do: to sit quietly, to accept without question whatever nonsense was inflicted on them, to ventriloquize on demand with a high degree of fidelity, to go down only on the down staircase, to speak only on signal from the teacher, and so on. All during these 16 years, they learned not to think, not to ask questions, not to figure things out for themselves. They learned to become totally dependent on teacher authority, and they learned it with dedication.

Naturally, this is what leads to the trouble when they are confronted with an opportunity to do what they must, to wit: make viable meanings in order to make, in turn, viable choices and decisions of their own, on their own.

Their first general reaction to the suggestion that *they* use the semester to formulate recommendations as to what they construe to be the best high-school experience for the nuclear space age is one of incredulity. They can't believe we're serious. They respond this way—while they don't realize it—because we have switched roles on them. They are all seated, notebooks open, pens poised, ready to "take notes" on "Problems and Practices in the Secondary School," in order to get some idea as to what this idiot professor thinks is important so that they can take the usual midsemester and final (multiple-choice) examinations with the high probability of "getting a good grade."

When they first become convinced that we are serious, things get worse. In their anxiety at having their academic Linus-blanket taken away, their first response is to attack us for refusing to "teach them anything," that is, for not having any "required texts," for not lecturing, and for not administering midterm and final (multiple-choice) examinations. Indeed, for "doing nothing"—other than asking them to invent "Quo Vadimus High School."

What we confront, at this juncture, is a most difficult problem in education: helping students to *unlearn* much of what they "know." Josh Billings said it almost a century ago: "The trouble ain't that people are ignorant; it's that they 'know' so much that ain't so." What are some of the things these students know that "ain't so"? Well, for example, they "know" that 1) the more "content" a person "knows," the better teacher he is; 2) that "content" is best "imparted" via a "course of study"; 3) that "content" is best kept "pure" by departmentalizing instruction; 4) that "content" or "subject matter" has a "logical structure" or "logical sequence" that dictates how the "content" should be "imparted"; 5) that bigger schools are better than smaller schools; 6) that smaller classes are better than bigger classes; 7) that "homogeneous grouping" (with students "grouped" on the basis of some real or fancied similarity) makes the learning of subjects more efficient; 8) that classes must be held for "periods" of about an hour in length, five days a week, for about 15 weeks in order for a "course" in a "subject" to happen.[1]

It comes as a shock to the students that there is *no evidence to support any of these contentions*. On the contrary, there is massive evidence to confute them. It takes some doing, however, to help students to recognize the fact that most of their deeply internalized assumptions about "education" are based on misinformation rather than information.

It is sometimes helpful for us to provide them with a set of beliefs in direct contradiction to those they hold. One of the

[1] See Ben M. Harris, "Ten Myths That Have Led Education Astray," *The Nation's Schools*, April 1962.

most dramatic comes from a highly personal statement by Carl Rogers. It appears in his book *On Becoming a Person*. In reviewing his experience as a teacher of teachers, Rogers concludes:

1. "My experience has been that I cannot teach another person how to teach."

2. "It seems to me that anything that can be taught to another is relatively inconsequential, and has little or no significant influence on behavior."

3. "I realize increasingly that I am only interested in learnings which significantly influence behavior."

4. "I have come to feel that the only learning which significantly influences behavior is self-discovered, self-appropriated learning."

5. "Such self-discovered learning, truth that has been personally appropriated and assimilated in experience, cannot be directly communicated to another."

6. "As a consequence of the above, I realize that I have lost interest in being a teacher."

Rogers goes on to state that the outcomes of trying to teach are either unimportant or hurtful and that he is interested only in being a learner. Some of our students react to this statement snidely, claiming that Rogers feels this way because he is a bad teacher. Honest, but bad. Others seem deeply disturbed by it and seek clarification on what Rogers means by "significant learning." We then produce Rogers' definition of the term, which is stated in the form of specific behaviors. They include:

The person comes to see himself differently.
He accepts himself and his feelings more fully.
He becomes more self-confident and self-directing.
He becomes more the person he would like to be.
He becomes more flexible, less rigid, in his perceptions.
He adopts more realistic goals for himself.
He behaves in a more mature fashion.
He becomes more open to the evidence, both of what is

going on outside of himself and of what is going on inside of himself.

Some of our students remain unmoved, preferring to believe that such behaviors, while important, are not fundamentally the concern of the teacher. But many students begin to modify their definitions of teaching and to reconsider what they want to do as teachers. Almost all take cognizance of the fact that *we*, at least, have planned no "curriculum" for them other than an inquiry into their own largely unexamined beliefs and assumptions.

The instrument of the inquiry is, of course, their development of "Quo Vadimus High School." As they proceed to produce such a school, many students feel a deep emotional involvement, largely, we think, because of their awareness of the fact that whatever they produce is going to represent a unique statement about themselves.

Some of the questions *they* find it necessary to ask in the process of formulating their recommendations for "Quo Vadimus High School" are:

1. What is the purpose of QVHS in the first place? What should it do? What kinds of students should it produce? What should the students be able to do when they leave that they could not do when they entered?

What objectives should QVHS have for itself and for its students? How can these objectives be "orchestrated" to enhance the possibility that QV's purpose will be fulfilled? What relationship to community and society is most desirable?

2. What are the students like? What do they know? What are their concerns? What is the world like from their point of view? How do they feel about it? What do they want to do in it—about it? What are the most important affectors of student attitudes, perceptions, assumptions, beliefs, values, choices? How conscious are they of the forces that affect them? What do they have in their repertoire of "survival

strategies"? What do they need to get rid of? Need to get better at? What do they need to add?

3. What "concepts" (attitudes, values, perspectives) must students master in order to be capable of the kinds of behavior that comprise the best forms of "coping" with the world in which they live? What "subjects" (if any) would be most useful in helping students to master these "concepts"?

4. What procedures and strategies would be most appropriate for helping students to master the concepts in number 3? What kind of an environment, setting, or atmosphere would be most conducive to internalizing these concepts rather than merely ventriloquizing them? What procedures should *NOT* be used? What atmosphere should *NOT* be permitted to develop? What might the physical setting of QV best be like? What kind of faculty and administration should QV have? What should student role and responsibility be in the overall operation of QV—whatever its physical form? What criteria might be used in selecting staff? How implement these criteria?

5. What kinds of procedures can QV students and staff develop and use to keep track of the degree to which QV is fulfilling its purpose? What kinds of procedures can QV use to make changes that appear necessary in response to "feedback"? What kinds of procedures should *NOT* be developed? What procedures might QV develop to deal with critical attacks on it, its purpose and procedures?

As the sample questions above suggest, there is an almost inexhaustible number of questions that can be asked even in a "simple" little process like inventing Quo Vadimus High School. Some groups of students even get into questions that lead them to invent a school motto, school songs, and school cheers for QV.

Almost every group of students that pursues this process comes up with a different version of Quo Vadimus High School. *At this stage in their metamorphosis* the process of invention is more important than the product invented. And, frankly, this is all we are interested in. If we can get a large group of our students engaged in the process of *asking* questions about what they are doing—about their assumptions, their metaphors, their language—then we feel satisfied that we have helped them to become creative agents in any new education that might be conceived. Indeed, we have found that in many, but not in all, instances, the students who go through this process are very different persons from the ones they were before posing—and answering, however tentatively—these previously unasked questions. How are they different? Well, it varies, but in general they have been freed from a dependence on arbitrary authority. They have greater respect for themselves as professionals because *they* are no longer mere functionaries willing to accept palpably inefficient and irrelevant bureaucratic rituals. They are anti-entropic agents ready to question (and provide alternative answers to) the attitudes in the schools that produce institutional inertia. They are agents of self-renewal. They are ready to *act as if* what is known about learning is true, rather than merely "pass a test" on it.

Goodwin Watson's summary [2] of what is known about learning, for example, is viewed by such students as a series of guidelines for inventing learning activities designed *not* to seduce students into learning inert ideas, but rather to help them gain mastery of new concepts necessary for survival in a world where precedent is the least useful source of analogy.

Watson's summary included the following "obvious" points:

1. Behavior which is rewarded—from the learner's point of view—is more likely to recur.

2. Sheer repetition without reward is a poor way to learn.

3. Threat and punishment have variable effects upon learning, but they can and do commonly produce avoidance behavior—in which the reward is the diminution of punishment possibilities. Punishment, it can be seen, is not the "opposite" of reward. Indeed, much of the activity the school uses as

[2] "What Do We Know About Learning?" *Teachers College Record*, 1960–61, pp. 253–257.

"punishment" is perceived by students as reward, and so rather than to eliminate the behavior being "punished" the school in fact reinforces it.

4. How "ready" we are to learn something new is contingent upon the confluence of diverse—and changing—factors, some of which Ames identified in his perception demonstration. Others include:

    a. adequate existing experience to permit the new to be learned (we can learn only in relation to what we already know);

    b. adequate significance and relevance for the learner to engage in learning activity (we learn only what is appropriate to our purposes);

    c. freedom from discouragement, the expectation of failure, or threats to physical, emotional, or intellectual well-being.

5. *Whatever* is to be learned will remain unlearnable if we believe that we cannot learn it or if we perceive it as irrelevant or if the learning situation is perceived as threatening.

6. Novelty (per 4 and 5 above) is generally rewarding.

7. We learn best that which we participate in selecting and planning ourselves.

8. Genuine participation (as compared with feigned participation intended to avoid punishment) intensifies motivation, flexibility, and rate of learning.

9. An autocratic atmosphere (produced by a dominating teacher who controls direction via intricate punishments) produces in learners apathetic conformity, various—and frequently devious—kinds of defiance, scapegoating (venting hostility generated by the repressive atmosphere on colleagues), or escape (psychologically or physically). An autocratic atmosphere also produces increasing dependence upon the authority, with consequent obsequiousness, anxiety, shyness, and acquiescence.

10. "Closed," authoritarian environments (such as are characteristic of most conventional schools and classrooms)

condemn most learners to continuing criticism, sarcasm, discouragement, and failure so that self-confidence, aspiration (for anything but escape), and a healthy self-concept are destroyed. Whitehead called this kind of a process "soul murder." Learners condemned to such relentless failure learn only that they cannot learn, and their anger and distress in the face of this is frequently vented against the system and the society that has inflicted this inhuman punishment on them.

11. The best time to learn anything is when whatever is to be learned is immediately useful to us.

12. An "open," nonauthoritarian atmosphere can, then, be seen as conducive to learner initiative and creativity, encouraging the learning of attitudes of self-confidence, originality, self-reliance, enterprise, and independence. All of which is equivalent to learning how to learn.

Now, here is the point we have been trying to make: prospective teachers cannot be "taught" to act on such knowledge as this unless their teachers act on that knowledge. The methods course we have been describing does not attempt to tell students what we think they ought to know. It attempts to have students do what we think they need to do within an environment that is based on what is known about learning. It is very important for us to say that many of the students who have been through such an experience demand, eventually, that we reveal to them sources of knowledge that have influenced us. When such demands are authentic—that is, when they are not attempts to avoid learning—we will provide students with a bibliography as respectable in length as any that "real" professors hand out in "real" courses. The list consists largely of the works of authors we have mentioned in this book. It will not surprise us if we should include, sometime soon, this book itself. But one must always be cautious about the efficacy of books. Al Smith once remarked that no young lady ever lost her virtue by reading a book. One might say with equal truth that no one ever became a good teacher by going through a bibliography. A woman loses her virtue by *doing* something she shouldn't; a student becomes a good teacher by doing something he should. Which brings us to a second point: if every college teacher "taught" his courses in the manner we have suggested, there would be no need for a methods course. Every course would then be a course in methods of learning and, therefore, in methods of teaching. For example, a "literature" course would be a course in the processes of learning how to read. A history course would be a course in the processes of learning how to *do* history. And so on. But this is the most farfetched possibility of all since college teachers, generally speaking, are more fixated on the Trivia game than any group of teachers in the educational hierarchy. Thus, we are left with the hope that, if methods courses could be redesigned to be model learning environments, the educational revolution might begin. In other words, it will begin as soon as there are enough young teachers who sufficiently despise the crippling environments they are employed to supervise to want to subvert them. The revolution will begin to be *visible* when such teachers take the following steps (many students who have been through the course we have described do not regard these as "impractical"):

1. Eliminate all conventional "tests" and "testing."
2. Eliminate all "courses."
3. Eliminate all "requirements."
4. Eliminate all full-time administrators and administrations.
5. Eliminate all restrictions that confine learners to sitting still in boxes inside of boxes.

We hope that, by now, you are using different criteria to judge what is practical, but if these suggestions still seem impractical to you, we need to say that the conditions we want to eliminate have not been selected whimsically. They just happen to be the sources of the most common obstacles to learning. We have largely trapped ourselves in our schools into expending almost all of our energies and resources in the direction of preserving patterns and procedures that make no sense *even in their own terms.* They simply do not produce the results that are claimed as their justification in the first place—quite the contrary.

If it is practical to persist in subsidizing at an ever-increasing economic and social cost a system which condemns our youth to ten or 12 or 16 years of servitude in a totalitarian environment ostensibly for the purpose of training them to be fully functioning, self-renewing citizens of a democracy, then we are vulnerable to whatever criticisms can be leveled. If, however, you feel it possible to agree that it is not "practical" to persist in this effort, perhaps we can spend some of our energies and resources on the invention of alternatives.

The elimination of conventional tests, for example, is necessary because, as soon as they are used as judgment-making instruments, the whole process of schooling shifts from education to training intended to produce passing grades on tests. About the only wholesome grounds on which mass testing can be justified is that it provides the conditions for about the only creative intellectual activity available to students—cheating. It is quite probable that the most original "problem solving" activity students engage in in school is related to the invention of systems for beating the system. We'd be willing to accept testing if it were *intended* to produce this kind of creativity.

"Courses" turn out to be contingent upon testing. A "course" generally consists of a series of briefings for the great Trivia contest. It's a kind of rigged quiz show. And it seems to work *only* if the participants value the "prize." The "prize," of course, is a "grade." An appropriate grade permits the participant to continue playing the Trivia game. All the while, let's not forget, very little, if any, substantive intellectual activity is going on.

Conventional "requirements" have to be abandoned because they, too, change the subject from education to something else. "Requirements" are systems of prescriptions and proscriptions intended solely to limit the physical and intellectual movements of students—to "keep them in line, in sequence, in order," etc. They shift the focus of attention from the learner (check Watson again) to "the course." In the process, "requirements" violate virtually everything we know about learning because they comprise the matrix of an elaborate system of punishments that, in turn, comprise a threatening atmosphere in which positive learning cannot occur. The "requirements," indeed, *force the teacher*—and administrator—into the role of an authoritarian functionary whose *primary* task becomes that of enforcing the requirements rather than helping the learner to learn. The whole authority of the system is contingent upon the "requirements."

Which gets us to "administrators." Administrators are another curious consequence of a bureaucracy which has forgotten its reason for being. In schools, administrators commonly become myopic as a result of confronting all of the problems the "requirements" generate. Thus, they cannot see (or hear) the constituents the system ostensibly exists to serve—the students. The idea that the school should consist of procedures specifically intended to help learners learn strikes many administrators as absurd—and "impractical." The nature of "administration" seems to insure this conclusion. Eichmann, after all, was "just an administrator." He was merely "enforcing requirements." The idea of "full-time administrators" is palpably a bad one—especially in schools—and we say to hell with it. Most of the "administration" of the school should be a student responsibility. If schools functioned according to the democratic ideals they pay verbal allegiance to, the students would long since have played a major role in developing policies and procedures guiding its operation. One of the insidious facts about totalitarianism is its seeming "efficiency." Responsibility *needs* to be delegated, and with it the authority to carry it out, BUT in order for a democratic system to work—however imperfectly —the responsible authority must be accountable to its constituents. In schools this means the students. Democracy—with all of its "inefficiency"—is still the best system we have so far for enhancing the prospects of our mutual survival. The schools must begin to act as if this were so.

Finally, it remains to be said that—as the world goes—about the last place any of us can expect to learn anything important about the realities we have to cope with in our wistful pursuit of life, liberty, and happiness is a classroom. If we decided that schools must do whatever was *necessary* to help students to learn the concepts and skills relevant to the nuclear space age, we wouldn't spend much time sitting inside of small boxes inside of big boxes—even with all of the fancy hardware being developed to jazz up the Trivia contest. It's probably true that most of what we all know we didn't learn in school anyway. Moreover, developments in electronic information processing make the school *as it presently exists* unnecessary. How about that? Which gets us back—again—to the "new education." Its purpose is to produce people who can cope effectively with change. To date, none of the new "educational technology" has that as its purpose. Remember Santayana's line: Fanaticism consists of redoubling one's efforts after having forgotten one's aim. The developments in "educational technology" are intended to do all of the old school stuff better—and they probably do, but that's not the aim of the new education.

We'd use all—or whatever is relevant at any particular juncture—of the emerging "educational technology," but only to help learners learn (*à la* Watson) strategies for survival in a changing world. This is the world to which the new education addresses itself. That's what's new about it, and that's why new kinds of teachers are needed to make it go.

IX. City Schools

CITY SCHOOLS as they now exist largely confine students to sitting in boxes with the choice of acquiescing to teacher demands or getting out.

Although it seems easy to disparage the observation that teachers with conventional middle-class attitudes cause most of the problems that they themselves deplore in schools, the testimony provided by students, both verbally and behaviorally, requires that this criticism be met. In the case of white teachers and Negro students, the dismissal of this criticism merely requires the dismissal of reality.

The very form and substance of conventional city schools, especially for "disadvantaged" students, *produces* the most commonly perceived problems. The problems are real, but they are not inevitable, because the process which produces them can be modified.

At present, the conventional school is a hostile place, especially to urban "disadvantaged" children. They do not learn what the school says it "teaches," and they drop out—or are

thrown out—of it as soon as they reach an age where this is
legally possible.

These "failures" do not disappear. They remain in the community, and they comprise an endless and growing population
dedicated to "getting even" with the society that has reviled
and rejected them in the school. The cost—just in dollars—we
pay for dealing with these drop- or push-outs far exceeds virtually *whatever* cost would be entailed in modifying the school
environment so as to produce attitudes and skills in these young
people that would help them to become participating and contributing members of the community rather than its enemies.

However "impractical and romantic" the following suggestions seem, they are certainly no more "impractical" than the
existing city schools which now contribute to the development
of the greatest source of threat to the existence of the city as a
viable community—its "disadvantaged" youth.

It is possible to view the "school" in the city, particularly in
"disadvantaged" areas, more as a *process* than as a structure.
There are many reasons for taking such a view, not the least of
which is that of changing the connotations that the school conventionally elicits. Furthermore, if the process is viewed as
having its primary objective the provision of direct and immediate service to the community, a number of otherwise
"invisible" potentials become apparent. For example, the
process could be structured around 1) identifying community
problems, 2) planning possible solutions on a variety of levels,
and 3) carrying out a plan the objective of which is to produce
some immediate and palpable amelioration of the problems.
In a way, such a school process permits the school to function
as a kind of local "think tank" with the intellectual activity
focused on problems the staff (students) identifies, and with
all of this reinforced by the physical activity entailed in carrying out the solutions.

Such a school process has the immediate community as its
"curriculum." School, in this sense, becomes a primary instrument for dealing in services and products which the community
needs.

There are no "subjects" in the conventional sense; the community and its problems and the students working to develop possible solutions embody all "subjects." The students—across all of the age ranges now found in school—are the primary action agents, and they are paid (rewarded) not merely with "grades," but with currency they value, including public recognition.

Adolescents, especially male dropouts, should have leadership responsibility throughout, with "teachers" playing a consultant or advisory role.

One of the functions of this kind of schooling is to open an avenue of constructive, responsible participation in community affairs to adolescents and young adults who are now usually denied such opportunity, and who, partly as a consequence, turn to anticommunity activities as an alternative.

This kind of schooling need not confine students to sitting in a classroom. The whole city can—and should—be a continuous "learning laboratory," with the immediate community as the source of immediate reward for all activity.

The services such a "school" might use as a vehicle include:

1. community planning and action programs, running from information services that could include newsletters, magazines, and films, to rat extermination, with a bounty paid for each rat killed, and awards for better approaches to the problem;

2. a range of services geared to immediate daily problems, including repair services for household appliances and equipment;

3. a range of "cultural" services, including student-produced musical and dramatic programs, puppet shows, films, television programs, etc., on a continuing basis; there could be a city-wide talent program with the best performers and performances being showcased on a weekly TV program, or in other community facilities;

4. a range of "athletic" services (possibly adjunct to the "cultural" program) again on a city-wide basis; this might

be of an "intramural" type, possibly under the aegis of a City Athletic Club, with a continuing round-robin series of contests; placing participants on an Olympic team might be one of the objectives of such a program;

5. a range of services in or to city agencies—hospitals, police, fire, sanitation, parks, museums, etc. (this might be extended into private business).

The school might also get into the production of stuff including clothing, food, and household and personal decorations. These products could be sold—or otherwise distributed—in the community. Students could operate vegetable and flower gardens as well as bakery, toy-repair, junk-conversion (even into "art"), millinery and dress, ceramics and jewelry, and photography shops, for example, with the whole merchandising process being added to the production process. Animal shelters and "pet libraries" could also be operated. The school process might even include a kind of *kibbutz* experience on public or privately owned land both inside and outside the city. The point to all of this is to give kids something constructive to *do* —and it could be on a continuing year-round basis, just like the rest of the community. Not only would the range of their kinesthetic experiences be widely increased, but the consequences of this would permit the development of "literacy" in a variety of ways conventional schools do not even admit exist. It probably needs to be emphasized that the foregoing is not a restatement of a plan of "vocational" education. We are suggesting here examples of a spectrum of activities addressed to community needs which could comprise a vehicle for a total education.

Private business and industry might be induced to provide "awards" in various forms to the students who participate in ways that ought to be recognized beyond the performance itself.

Arrangements could probably be worked out with public and private colleges and universities to admit students from such a school system on the basis of performance in these activities rather than on the basis of "grades" in conventional "subjects."

Arrangements could also be made with various business enterprises in the city and state to provide some kind of "apprentice" opportunity at various points in the program. It might not be necessary to send students out in all cases, since business and industry could provide some "consultants" to assist students engaged in some activity they need help with.

Such a school process, then, has as its primary function the development of responsible community leadership through providing students with the opportunity for substantive participation in the invention, initiation, and implementation of programs intended to improve the community. This, in turn, produces various effects, including 1) freeing students from detention in a school that virtually insures their alienation from the community at large, and 2) minimizing the continuation of bureaucratic agencies populated by functionaries who are not part of the community ostensibly to be served. Such a process also would have the effect of channeling the energies and abilities of young (particularly male) adolescents into constructive rather than destructive directions. It could also produce a viable political network by maintaining direct communication with the community through its youth, thus minimizing the proliferation of competing "spokesmen" and organizations, especially from sources outside the local community.

A school system of this type has the potential for becoming one of the most useful social-political instruments possible for dealing fruitfully with the problems of the city as they presently exist and as it seems they will probably develop in the future.

In such a system you do not need school structures as they presently exist, nor school "curricula" as they presently exist, nor school faculties as they presently exist. Whatever the reasons were for the present form of public schools, they have little or nothing to do with the problems that the city faces now, and so they need to be changed. If *any* publicly supported institution does not help to resolve problems as they really exist, why have it at all?

X. New Languages: The Media

ONE OF McLuhan's important contributions to the new education is his extension of the Sapir-Whorf Hypothesis.

As we have said, this is the view that language structures our perception of "reality." McLuhan and his colleague in media studies, anthropologist Edmund Carpenter, have suggested that the new electric media of communication comprise new languages.

When this idea is combined with the essential (and traditional) function of schools to develop literacy and sophistication in the languages (media) most important to the students, then media study becomes critical in the new education. The fact that the new media are inseparable from the changes occurring in the environment requires that the school's virtually exclusive concern with print literacy be extended to include these new forms; in other words, the magnitude of the effect of new media, still in the process of being assessed, requires that any attempt to increase the relevance of education include substantive consideration of them.

Let us, briefly, try to present a perspective on media change. Speech was not only the first instrument of mass communication, but, even more important, was the means by which man decisively and qualitatively differentiated himself from all other forms of life. More than the tool-making animal, man is the symbolizing animal. By definition, there is no human tradition older than the oral tradition.

Practically nothing is known about the origins of language except that men adapted organs of breathing and eating to the purpose of talking and have probably been making meaningful sounds at each other for at least 100,000 years. Although speech continues to be the most widely used symbolic device among men, as well as their basic mechanism of social integration, it is difficult for any of us to imagine a world in which speech serves as the only practice of language. For Western civilization, that world ended with the invention of the alphabet.

Our alphabet was invented by the Syrio-Palestinian Semites about 1500 B.C. and was carried to completion by the Phoenicians. Whereas speech is a primary or direct symbolization of events, processes, and things in the world, alphabetic writing is a set of symbols of a set of symbols; that is, an attempt to represent the sounds of human speech by a system of graphic signs. Through writing, the continuous flow of sounds that is speech was captured, as by a camera, and made motionless. In so doing man extended his language beyond the "natural" limitations of time and space. At first, man struggled with his new invention, affixing signs to almost any surface that could retain them with some degree of permanence. He tried, at one time or another, stone, bark, wax, bronze, clay, leather, papyrus, and vellum, on which surfaces he scratched, chiseled, or hammered. By the middle of the fourth century B.C., the Ionic alphabet of 24 letters had become standardized, and the portable and unpretentious papyrus scrolls of the Greeks were the best instrument for recording and preserving human speech that had yet emerged. Nevertheless, this transmutation of language did not meet with uniform approval. One of the facts that invariably emerges from any study of human communication is that anxiety, suspicion, and pessimism accompany communication changes. Men tend to resent the intrusion of a new medium of communication and often feel compelled to defend the older medium against anticipated or actual competition. Socrates, for example, wrote no books and believed that they were inferior to the spoken word as a means of education. In Plato's *Phaedrus* several significant passages express Socrates' hostility to the written word. The following is among the most familiar:

> A terrible thing about writing, Phaedrus, is this, and here, in truth, it is like painting. I mean, the creations of the painter stand like living creatures, but if you ask them anything, they maintain a solemn slience. And so it is with writings; you might think they spoke as if they had intelligence, but if you put a question with a wish for information on a point in what is said, there is one, one only, invariable reply. Further, once a word is written, it goes rolling all about, comes indifferently among those who understand it and all those whom it no wise concerns, and is unaware to whom it should address itself and to whom it should not do so.

But private prejudice is not a persevering antagonist to the movement of history. The invention of writing produced a chain of more or less radical reactions at almost every level of society. Writing, for instance, favored the progress of commerce; and light writing materials, in particular, led to the expansion of city-states into empires. Writing also tended to fix historical tradition and strengthen social cohesion. It encouraged an interest in science, contributed toward the development of Roman law, and facilitated the spread of Christianity.

On the other hand, throughout the entire period of "unmechanized" writing—from the clay tablet to the handwritten book—the spoken word remained preeminent. It was the main instrument of instruction, political persuasion, and literary experience. Homer's poetry was invariably recited. Herodotus publicly read his histories. One school of philosophy—Stoicism —was named after the porches from which its advocates talked. Cicero, the greatest of Roman orators, composed his speeches by saying them, and only later did he write them down. In fact, most of classical literature—poetry, drama, philosophy, history—was intended to be heard rather than read. Even well into the medieval period, language was essentially a medium of the ear, and almost all organized learning, both in and out of the school, was received by auditory methods. For all practical purposes, students had no sources of information or ideas other than the spoken words of their teachers. Written assignments and written examinations were unknown. There was no such thing as a slate or a blackboard. When students read from manuscripts, their pace was apparently extremely slow, even tortuous, as they "spelled" their way through each sheet somewhat in the manner of the uneducated reader of today. In short, the spoken word was the main channel of communication even in the face of competition from the handwritten manuscript. Not until the invention of print did another linguistic medium drastically intrude on man's symbolic consciousness.

The exact year and place in which the printing press of Western civilization was invented is somewhat in doubt. Seven cities, in fact, have claimed the honor, each fixing the date at a time different from the others. But it is generally accepted that Johannes Gensfleisch zum Gutenberg, a printer from the city of Mainz in Germany, produced the first "artificial script" in the year 1456 or 1457. This was the famous and still extant 42-line Bible. Before the century was over, in almost every country in Europe, books were being printed, as Gutenberg put it, "without the help of reed, stylus, or pen but by the wondrous agreement, proportion, and harmony of punches and types."

Printing was, from its beginning, a successful commercial venture. The new medium had no such formidable adversary as Socrates. Resistance to it came largely from those who had collected expensive libraries of manuscripts or those whose livelihood depended on manuscripts, namely, writers of manuscript. For the latter, the printing press was, so to speak, the handwriting on the wall.

Print, in even more revolutionary ways than writing, changed the very form of civilization. It is not entirely coincidence, for instance, that the Protestant Reformation was contemporaneous with the invention of movable type. From the time Martin Luther posted his theses in 1517, the printing press was used to publish controversial, even inflammatory, religious tracts. But even more important, the printing and distribution of millions of Bibles made possible a more personal religion, as the Word of God rested on each man's kitchen table.

The book, by isolating the reader and his responses, tended to separate him from the powerful oral influences of his family, teacher, and priest. Print thus created a new conception of self as well as of self-interest. At the same time, the printing press provided the wide circulation necessary to create national literatures and intense pride in one's native language. Print thus promoted individualism on the one hand and nationalism on the other.

Printing also created new literary forms and altered ideas of literary style. Medieval poetry was conceived for the ear, and each poem had to stand the test of recitation. In addition, medieval audiences were not always interested in the poet himself, since his work was known to them only through the interpretations of minstrels, who frequently rephrased poems to suit their own image and images. The printed page changed these conditions. Slowly, the printed poet came into a new relationship with his reader. He learned not to be so repetitive as his predecessors since a reader could be depended upon to return as often as needed to uncomprehended passages. He learned also to create rhymes and syntax for the eye as well as the ear, as John Donne did in his sermons. The form of the printed page itself provided a visual means of differentiating poetry from prose and added new dimensions to the art of versification. Prose assumed new forms, such as the personal essays of Montaigne and the novels of Defoe and Richardson, the last of whom was himself a printer. After the flowering of dramatic poetry during the Elizabethan Age, the printed page substituted for the theater, and millions of schoolchildren came to know Shakespeare only through this form.

In schools, print shifted the emphasis from oral to written and visual communication. Teachers who had been only partly concerned with instructing their students in how to read became by mid-sixteenth century concerned with almost nothing else. Since the sixteenth century, the textbook has been a primary source of income for book publishers. Since the sixteenth century, written examinations and written assignments have been an integral part of the methodology of school teaching; and since the sixteenth century, the image of the isolated student, the student who reads and studies by himself, has been the essence of our conception of scholarship. In short, for 400 years Western civilization has lived in what has been characterized as the "Age of Gutenberg." Print has been the chief means of our information flow. Print has shaped our literature and conditioned our responses to literary experience. Print has influenced our conception of the educational process.

Certainly printed media and the printed book in particular will continue to exert powerful influences on our society. Once they have become literate, most people have intellectual and emotional powers that are irrevocable. But equally certain is the fact that print no longer "monopolizes man's symbolic environment," to use David Riesman's phrase. That monopoly began to dissolve toward the middle of the nineteenth century, when a more or less continuous stream of media inventions began to make accessible unprecedented quantities of information and created new modes of perception and qualities of aesthetic experience. To select a specific year as marking the beginning of the "technological revolution" is difficult; but 1839 is probably the best. In that year, Daguerre developed the first practical method of photography. In 1844, Morse perfected the telegraph. In 1876, Bell transmitted the first telephone message. A year later, Edison invented the phonograph. By 1894, the movies had also been introduced. A year after that, Marconi sent and received the first wireless message. In 1906, Fessenden transmitted the human voice by radio. In 1920, regularly scheduled radio broadcasts began. In 1923, a picture was televised between New York and Philadelphia. In that same year, Henry Luce and Briton Hadden created a totally new idea in magazines with *Time*. In 1927, the first "talkie" appeared; and in 1928, Disney's first animated cartoon. In 1935, Major E. H. Armstrong developed the FM radio. In 1936 came *Life* magazine. In 1941, full commercial television was authorized. These are just some of the inventions that form a part of the "communications revolution" through which we are all living. To these could be added, of course, the LP record, the tape recorder, the comic strip, the comic book, the tabloid newspaper, the electronic computer, the paperback book.

Note that the point here is not that the "content" alone of these need be studied, but rather that the perceptual-cognitive effects on us of the *form* of these new languages be understood.

The way to be liberated from the constraining effects of any medium is to develop a perspective on it—how it works and what it does. Being illiterate in the processes of any medium (language) leaves one at the mercy of those who control it.

The new media—these new languages—then are among the most important "subjects" to be studied in the interests of survival. But they must be studied in a new way if they are to be *understood,* they must be studied as mediators of perception. Indeed, for any "subject" or "discipline" to be *understood* it must be studied this way.

As McLuhan has put it:

> All forms of mathematics and science, as much as the changing modes of historiography and literature, offer instruments and models of perception. It follows that any existing "subject" in our curricula can now be taught as a more or less minor group of models of perception favored in some past or at present. Taught in this way any "subject" becomes an organic

portion of almost any other "subject." Moreover, it also follows that "subject" taught structurally in this way offers innumerable opportunities for new perception and new insight even at elementary levels. The idea of the "content" of education as something to be lodged in the mind as a container thus belongs to the preelectronic phase and to the era of Euclidean space and Newtonian mechanics. A structure cannot be contained. Any conceivable container is at once part of the structure, modifying the whole. The idea of "content" at once reveals a structure of perception and assumptions from which the artist and the poet have been trying to free us for a full century. But now the nuclear physicist has intervened on the side of the artists, and the pressure to heed the message of the artists has become more urgent.

It was Whitehead's *Science and the Modern World* that first drew wide attention to the close relations between art and science. Any structural approach in education has to take into account his observations about structural procedures of the nineteenth century:

> The greatest invention of the nineteenth century was the invention of the method of invention. A new method entered into life. In order to understand our epoch, we can neglect all the details of change, such as railways, telegraphs, radios, spinning machines, synthetic dyes. We must concentrate on the method in itself; that is the real novelty which has broken up the foundations of the old civilization. . . . One element in the new method is just the discovery of how to set about bridging the gap between the scientific ideas, and the ultimate product. It is a process of disciplined attack upon one difficulty after another. [A. N. Whitehead, *Science and the Modern World*, New York: Macmillan Company, 1926, p. 141.]

The method of invention, as Edgar Poe demonstrated in his "Philosophy of Composition," is simply to begin with the solution of the problem or with the effect intended. Then one backtracks, step by step, to the point from which one must begin in order to reach the solution or effect. Such is the method of the detective story, of the symbolist poem, and of modern science. It is, however, the twentieth-century step beyond this method of invention which is needed for understanding the origin and the action of such forms as the wheel or the alphabet. And that step is not the backtracking from *product* to starting point, but the following of *process* in isolation from product. To follow the contours of process, as in psychoanalysis, provides the only means of avoiding the product of process, namely neurosis or psychosis.

The nineteenth-century discovery of the method of invention was the ultimate stage of the mechanical genius of our Western world that began with the alphabet and ended with the assembly line. To have isolated this process from its mere products, we owe to the artists and not to the scientists. However, we have now gone beyond the technique of the method of invention. It is the unique achievement of the twentieth century to have discovered the technique of the suspended judgment. That means the technique of understanding process in such a way as to avoid its consequences. We can now avoid "closure" because we understand it, in some areas at least. Perhaps this is akin to "weightlessness," the bypassing of gravitational consequences of a false step, as in a trick movie. And such understandi ng of process with the attendant means of evading its conse uences is a natural feature of the simultaneous "field." For, in "field" awareness, the effects are seen at the moment as the cause.[1]

In a world of high-speed, complex, simultaneous, total-field change, the conventional pedestrian academic mode of analytic, linear segmentation and explication itself comprises a threat to our survival.

The processes of the new education must replicate those of the real total-field world if students are to learn—in order to use—the concepts that comprise a "field awareness."

The new education will bear as little resemblance to the old as a space capsule bears to a stern-wheel riverboat, and for similar reasons.

It obviously makes no sense in trying to build a vehicle for

[1] Marshall McLuhan, "We Need a New Picture of Knowledge," *New Insights and the Curriculum*, A.S.C.D. Yearbook 1963 (NEA, Washington, D.C.).

a mission in space to use the blueprints, materials, and terminology appropriate to building a steamboat.

While it isn't so obvious yet, it makes no more sense to try to build the new education for its mission in the nuclear space age using the blueprints, materials, and terminology of the old education.

We have new languages to learn if we don't want to talk ourselves to death.

XI. Two Alternatives

AT ONE TIME OR ANOTHER (including the present), the ideas we have been proposing have been tried in one place or another, with almost all of the desirable results claimed for them being verified. The new education would simply consist of having all of them tried all of the time everywhere.

The following article, "Education and Reality," is by Frank Miceli, formerly Consultant for the Department of Education, Virgin Islands of the United States. His description of a "reality curriculum" presents in concrete terms some of the processes and concepts we have been talking about, and provides one illustration of the new education in action. (For another example of this kind of approach, see Terry Borton's article, "What Turns Kids On?" *Saturday Review*, April 15, 1967. Mr. Borton describes the development of a "questions curriculum" similar in many respects to what we have proposed.)

EDUCATION AND REALITY

by Frank Miceli

Teachers don't work with materials. They work with what they have in their heads and with what their students have in *their* heads. When the schooling process breaks down—that is, when students drop out—we can almost be sure that the origin of the failure is in the fact that the stuff in the teacher's head bore an inadequate relationship to the stuff in the learner's head. The student who believes that schooling offers him an opportunity to achieve material success will become a psychic dropout when there is a lack of congruence between his stuff and the teacher's stuff. The others just leave. Or make trouble.

When I worked in the Virgin Islands, I observed a program on St. Croix, at the College of the Virgin Islands. The program was designed to assist high-school students in studying aspects of life *they* wished to know more about. The program had been in existence for two years when I first learned of it. I spent five months studying how it worked, and I am convinced that it offers those of us in education a workable model for developing viable curricula (read: relevant stuff to do) for the future. For all kids.

First, the students: All the participants were volunteers. This was an "extracurricular" program—an important point, because it was relatively free of the usual administrative requirements that so often corrupt the learning process. Almost all the students had deficiencies in reading and writing (at least as judged by their local high-school teachers). All levels of academic achievement were represented in the total group of 80, from some college-bound students to many potential high-school dropouts.

The staff based its activities on two curious assumptions. The first was a belief that the classroom was a stage on which students, not teachers, should perform. The second was the belief that the students should feel that they were learning something. The latter assumption had more immediate practical significance than the former because, if the students did not see the value of the sessions, they would not attend. And that would be the end of the program. And the teachers.

The description that follows represents my close observations of the communication section of the program.

The instructor spent the first few sessions (three hours per session) eliciting from the students questions they were concerned to know more about. In other words, they were asked to think about questions that they thought were worth answering. Now, whenever students are asked to think about questions (as against answers), the response is the same. They do not regard the activity as serious. (This fact, by itself, constitutes a devastating indictment against our conventional schooling process.) Nonetheless, the instructor accommodated the rather lighthearted attitude of his students by introducing what he called "the black attaché-case game." It went like this: The instructor brought to class a black attaché case. He told the students that inside the case there was a small computer which was capable of producing the answer to any question anyone asked. "What questions," he asked, "do you want it to answer?" Dozens of questions came:

> When was I born?
> What is my mother's maiden name?
> What should we do about Vietnam?
> Why are grown-ups always angry at teenagers?
> Why can't we grade ourselves in school?
> If everyone makes H-bombs, won't someone drop one some day?
> If love is dead, why do I feel so great with my boyfriend?
> How many miles is it from St. Croix to San Francisco?

And so on.

The instructor then informed the class that the computer was expensive to operate and that it would be wasteful to use it on questions to which the answers were already known. The students examined their list and eliminated from it those questions whose answers could easily be given (e.g., "When was I born?" "What is my mother's maiden name?"). Next, the instructor told the students that the computer had trouble with questions that were vaguely phrased. Unless the computer knew exactly what was *meant* by the words in the question, its answers would be confusing. For example, in the question "What should we do about Vietnam?" what is meant by "we"? What is meant by "should"? Is it a "moral should"? Is it a "political should"? In the question "How many miles is it from St. Croix to San Francisco?" what is meant by "miles"? Air miles? Ship miles? And so on.

Here is what happened during a three-week period of the black attaché-case game: Of course, the students quickly realized that there was no miraculous computer in the case. They were only slightly disappointed. (They did insist, for some reason, that the black case be *physically* present at every session.) They came to class every meeting and expressed repeatedly the opinion that what was going on was worthwhile. They evolved a list of questions to ask about questions. They came to believe that their question list was a powerful instrument in helping someone to know *a)* what he is talking about, *b)* what sort of information he wants, *c)* whether or not a question can be answered, and *d)* what he must do to find an answer if one *can* be found. As might have been predicted, the students felt that what they had been doing was not "school stuff." They were asked, "What is it about?" A student replied, Thinking."

After these sessions, the instructor began a "writing" phase of the program by asking the students to write him a letter dealing with any questions or problems or things they felt strongly about. He told them he would write a letter back to them. The students did not know how to react to the teacher. One girl raised her hand and asked if the teacher would read the letters aloud in class. He said he would not, that the letters would be personal communications between them, and that he would respond not with short notes, but with detailed replies. "Would you tell us in your letter about things that bother *you?*" asked one student. The teacher said he would: "However, I'll only write what bothers me if you promise not to correct my spelling." The students laughed. "Besides, if I write and ask you something, if I have a question for you, will you respond with a letter to me?" The class laughed again, even louder. They thought he was kidding. Students always think "real stuff" is not serious.

During the next month or so, letters were exchanged frequently. That is, ideas and feelings were exchanged, and never once was the word "composition" mentioned. Teachers should give that some thought. When was the last time *you* wrote a "composition"? Outside of the separate life of a school, when does anyone put pen to paper to write a composition? And if compositions bear no relationship to reality, why continue to assign them? Why not letters as a way of getting students to talk? Of course, we would have to answer the letters, to *talk back,* to respond not only to the mechanical quality of the student's writing, but also to what he has to say to us.

The grammar and spelling of the students improved in the *process* of communicating with the instructor, as a function of what the students had to say, and not in the vacuum of a workbook. The situation was congruent with reality. The curriculum became the stuff of curiosity, the threads of a fabric two people weave when they talk to each other. Not all the students wrote about themselves. Some didn't need to. But all began to see some special quality in writing, some magic in words, that they had never seen before. And the teacher became aware of a special dimension in education that, on a large scale, has never been explored or studied: what the *teacher* has to say of a personal and compelling nature to students.

If you are a teacher, when was the last time you wrote something to a pupil so that he could comment on *your* ideas? Don't you think a school year ought to be a continuing exchange of ideas, rather than a series of staccato "lessons" and "units"? But perhaps teachers have nothing to communicate to students. Perhaps they are afraid to talk with them. Maybe that's what lesson plans are all about—a tactical diversion so that no one need *say* anything to anyone.

The instructor in the communication section kept careful records of what happened during all the three-hour sessions. The descriptions of what actually occurred were matched against the plans for what was supposed to happen. The plans for each session grew out of an analysis of the kinds of questions the students were concerned about in class and in their letters. An overwhelming proportion of questions dealt with the students' fear of social rejection, the tenuousness of friendship, sexual exploration, breaking away from parental control, and success in college or in a job. Many feared immaturity; some feared our involvement in Vietnam. The teacher needed to be very wise and to know a great deal. If his letters were fatuous, the students told him so.

On one occasion, the students were asked by the instructor to respond in writing to the questions and statements below. The only instruction given the students was that they were not to write in complete sentences, but to respond in three-, four-, or five-word phrases. If a particular question did not interest them, or if nothing occurred to them, they were to omit the question:

1. What do you hear if you are in a car and it is raining outside? What do you feel if you are standing outside?
2. Describe the odor of gasoline.
3. What sounds do you hear if you are walking with heavy boots in a deep snow? (Don't use the word "crunch.")
4. What does hair feel like? Anybody's hair
5. Describe the texture of skin. Feel it.
6. How would you describe fear? If you've never been afraid, don't answer. If you have, you don't have to answer either, unless you want to.
7. Describe the odor of freshly cut grass.
8. Describe the sensation of placing an ice cube against your lips.

9. Is there a particular odor in the air before a rainfall? Describe it.

10. Is there a particular odor in the air after a rainfall? Describe it.

11. If your hand slides across a piece of silk, what sensation do you feel?

12. If you were to walk barefoot along a beach of pebbles, what would you feel?

13. What does your hand feel like?

14. What does someone else's hand feel like?

15. Describe the taste of salt.

16. Describe the flight of a seagull.

When the answers had been written, the instructor asked for volunteers to share them, and selected one girl. She went to the board and wrote her responses. She was asked to write them without identifying numbers, so that it would look as if they were all of a piece, not 16 different reactions. What she wrote is reproduced, unedited, below.

Soft rhythms on tin
Torrents of miniwetness
Odor spray
Spreading, pushing, never toe touching ground
Twisting strands—sometimes silky flowing, oil
Smooth body surface
Filled with dread anticipation
Moist flower fragrance
A burning cold
Wet heat, when first to breathe is dying
In fresh clearance objects sparkle and air is pure
A finely never broken woven texture
Sharp, bumpy pains against the pad of feet
Dry dampness underneath
Bare-top dry
Blue crystals on tongue
All perfection, soaring through air with wings
Outstretched, silhouetted against the cloud.

As the student wrote her reactions on the board, the instructor asked several students in their seats to read aloud their responses, as if they were part of a whole, and not fragments. After several were read aloud, the instructor turned the attention of the class to the responses on the board. He read the responses aloud.

INSTRUCTOR: What does that sound like?
FIRST STUDENT: Some kind of poetry.
SECOND STUDENT: Free verse.
INSTRUCTOR: How can that be?

[*No response.*]

Why should a group of reactions sound like poetry?
THIRD STUDENT: Because the same person wrote them.
INSTRUCTOR: But what makes it hang together?

[*No response.*]

It does hang together, doesn't it?

The students were soon saying that people write out of a well-integrated web of experiences and, no matter what they write, regardless of the descriptions, their phrases would seem to go together because "a person is together." They went on to formulate tentative hypotheses about personality integration, prose, poetry, how one writes, how one reads, and the difficulty a person who is "not together" would have with reading and writing. When asked if they had liked what they had written, the students answered with a unanimous "Yes." When asked if they would like to write a poem, they answered with a unanimous "No."

INSTRUCTOR: But you enjoyed the writing in class.
FIRST STUDENT: You didn't say it was a poem.
SECOND STUDENT: You tricked us.
INSTRUCTOR: May I trick you some more?

[*Laughter.*]

It is important to say here that the curriculum that emerged in these classes had a curious but compelling unity. The students did a great deal of writing and talking. They asked dozens of questions about language, some of which were strikingly original. They also asked many questions of an intensely personal nature. And they came every day. Not because they were required to come, but because they felt that what was happening had something to do with them. When they were asked, "What subject are we studying?" they thought the question odd. One student said, "Well, it's not a subject, exactly. It's more like group therapy." Another said, "The subject is me." Still another, "Subjects are what you study in school. This is something else." The "subject," of course, *was* them: that is, it concerned *their* perceptions of the world, and their attempts to communicate with that world. For this reason, each session was not only intensely interesting, in a way that school seldom is, but each session was also connected with the previous one by virtue of its *psychological continuity*. The curriculum was not a logical sequence of predetermined pieces of something. It was a flow of ideas, one idea leading to the next because that was the order in which the students thought them. The instructor never had occasion to say, "Today we will discuss . . ." The students always knew what they were to discuss because, in a sense, the discussion of the previous lesson had not ended.

I want to raise a few questions here about the word "subject." What *is* a subject? Are subjects "things"? ("Have you taken economics?" "Why, no." "You should study *it*.") Do subjects grow? If they do, how? Where do subjects reside? In books? In people's heads? Why are students required to study subjects? Do young children think in terms of subjects? If not, why are they such curious, persistent learners?

I don't know the answers to these questions, but I have the impression that we need to ask ourselves about these matters if we want to break new ground in education. In any case, the program I am describing did not look like any "subject" I had seen before in school. And that fact made a big, positive difference to the students. For example, some of the questions raised by the instructor during the course of the term were these:

1. Is there any moral or legal relationship between fooling around with marijuana, fooling around with someone else's wife or husband, and fooling around with an income-tax return?
2. Why do people like to buy items made of plastic? What does it say about them? What does it say about plastic?
3. What does it mean to you that most families have a bathroom cabinet filled with small bottles of drugs?
4. If you want to say something without using words, how would you go about it? Is there a silent language?
5. Why are people who love each other sometimes cruel to each other?

Some of the questions the students raised were:

1. Why do we have such a thing as a "dirty word"?
2. Why do I fear certain words?
3. Do people kill each other over words?
4. Should people kill each other over words?
5. Who knows most about how words work? Teachers? Advertisers? Politicians?
6. Why do people pray?
7. Why do people yell at each other?

Not every one of these questions was discussed, but most were. And in discussing them, the students brought to bear what they had read, what they had seen, and what they had felt. In short, they were educating themselves in an environment that allowed the world to enter.

If more and more students become less and less interested in what we have to offer them, we will, I believe, begin to discover by default what our profession is all about, and what it should have been from the beginning: the study of how students learn by asking and being asked relevant questions. The student must be central in any curriculum development.

Not central to the limit that we bear him in mind as we construct *our* intellectual houses, but central in that our curricula begin with what he feels, cares about, fears, and yearns for. Most curricula are concerned with the structure of the comfortable past. We had here a curriculum concerned with the here and now, the difficult present, and more teachers should prepare themselves for confrontations with students who, rightfully, want a program that is part of our new world and has a vital place in it for them. If we can say that all human discovery, regardless of discipline, starts with an answerable question, then we ought to look at the curriculum as a series of questions from students that the school helps them to explore—regardless of how indelicate those questions might be. Any curriculum, after all, ought to recognize the existence of the real world.

The new education can be achieved in a number of ways. The processes we are interested in can be developed through a questions curriculum, a systems curriculum, or even a games curriculum. Although the word "game" has connotations that are not usually associated with intellectual growth, there are few concepts or skills that could not be learned with a rare degree of understanding and durability through an educational-game approach. In fact, a "game approach" permits the development of a learning environment that is much more congruent to what we know about learning than any other approach now used in schools. The teacher's role—in a "game" —shifts from that of the single, autocratic authority or opponent to that of a consultant or coach—a helper. The "game" also eliminates the unwholesome cutthroat "competition" for a single, abstract, and externally imposed "reward"—a grade. In a game approach, cooperation among "team" members— largely in formulating inductively a range of viable alternatives to real problems that comprise the process of the game —permits the development of concepts that are appropriate, rather than inimical, to the fostering of human survival processes.

The prototypes for such educational games now exist. They are *not* played "to win." They are not "simple," and they do not rely primarily on chance, although, as is the case in all human situations, "chance" plays a part. But then, we need a new concept of "chance," too, and these games can help to develop it.

"Games" of the kind we have in mind can be used at any "grade level" and for learning any concept. The basic process of such a game is the replication of some aspect of the human condition in microcosm in order to confront the "players" with problems requiring the "discovery" of viable alternative solutions. In almost no case is there ever a single possible solution. It all depends—upon all of the stuff suggested by us earlier in this book. "Games" could easily comprise the basis for most learning systems. They would encourage a relatively "uncontaminated" learning environment in which the school and the teachers are flexible *resources* for probing new questions. Such an environment could transform the school into what it should be—a learning laboratory.

The following article by Elliott Carlson of *The Wall Street Journal* describes, we think, some of the interesting possibilities that a "games" curriculum might offer.

GAMES IN THE CLASSROOM

by Elliott Carlson

More than 200 high-school students from 20 states will descend on Nova High School in Ft. Lauderdale, Florida, this month for the school's second annual Olympic games. But the activities at Nova's sumptuous spread—part of the 545-acre South Florida Education Center—will have little to do with the usual athletic exertions conjured by the word "Olympics." Instead, Olympic participants will shun the rigors of the track for the comforts of the classroom: They will play Equations, a mathematics game devised by a Yale law professor, in an experiment to determine whether a spate of newly developed strategy games can have an influence on the adolescent as pervasive as that of athletic programs.

Recognizing that high-school athletes generally are accorded recognition and prestige by their peers while scholars are less "acceptable," Robert W. Allen, director of Nova's two-year-old Academic Games Project, declares that the Nova Olympics are aimed at restructuring this "value perspective." In time, through competitive use of a panoply of games, Mr. Allen hopes the school achievement of adolescents will be improved by "altering the structure of values and rewards evidenced in many schools."

Although Nova is the only school to make such games the focus of a national championship, it is by no means alone in discovering their educational possibilities. A growing number of schools—universities as well as secondary and elementary schools—are finding that various problem-solving games can be helpful in teaching everything from mathematics and business administration to international relations.

Hastening entry of the sometimes controversial games into secondary and elementary schools is mounting teacher dissatisfaction with old-fashioned textbook approaches to course material. Some Baltimore and San Diego high schools have found that games can help motivate slow learners. And grade schools in northern Westchester County, New York, working under a U.S. Office of Education grant, have designed games to teach sixth-graders the economic problems of an emerging nation and the operation of a retail toy store.

On the university level, the same spirit of innovation is infecting a growing number of graduate schools of business, where some educators contend games may remedy a deficiency in those curriculums overlooking that decision making occurs in a context of conflict. Four years ago, the University of Chicago's Graduate School of Business introduced a game reflecting the workings of the international trade system.

About the same time the Harvard Business School introduced a game for first-year graduate students simulating a consumer-goods industry. Last year the University of Pennsylvania's Wharton School of Finance and Commerce introduced a similar game. In all, some 50 university business schools make use of management games, about double the number in 1963, according to one estimate. Business schools by no means monopolize games, however. At Northwestern University, the University of Michigan, and a sprinkling of other colleges, political-science students play a game called Inter-Nation Simulation, which supplements courses in international relations.

While it is all the rage in some schools, there is, to be sure, nothing new about gaming itself. War games are as old as gladiators and jousting knights, who used them to develop alternative tactics and strategies. Since the mid-seventeenth century, when a group of Prussian generals adapted chess for an exercise called the King's Game, games played on tabletops have provided a respectable means for the study of war and maneuver. But it wasn't until 1956 that a nonmilitary strategy game was devised. Spurred by the growing availability of computers, the American Management Association put together the first widely known management-training game. Soon afterward, games found their way into the university and business communities. Despite their modern complexity, which would have dazzled the Prussian generals, researchers concede that the value of educational games has yet to be established. Nevertheless, the exercises are being used for a bewildering array of purposes by firms, hospitals, labor unions, and even the State Department, which uses them to study counterinsurgency problems. It is in the schools, however, where the games are most varied and where their use may prove most rewarding.

Why are games considered effective learning aids? For one thing, "they spur motivation," claims Kalman J. Cohen, professor of economics and industrial administration at the Carnegie Institute of Technology, which began pioneering in games as early as 1958. "Students get very absorbed in the competitive aspects of the game. They try harder at games than in some courses." More important, he adds, the exercises "give students an opportunity to practice decision-making techniques or approaches studied in the classroom. They force students to live with the consequences of their decisions, an experience hard to get in the classroom."

Typical of business games is Carnegie Tech's, developed to realistically mirror the problems of running a company. The purpose of the game, which involves about 18 graduate-student "executives" representing three competing firms in a fictional detergent industry, is almost breathtakingly ambitious. Dr. Cohen says it is aimed at providing guided experience in managerial decision making under conditions of competition and uncertainty. At the same time, he says, the game seeks to advance student skills of analysis, advocacy, and negotiation in contacts with outside groups, such as boards of directors, bankers, and union representatives.

As the game gets underway, players huddle over charts and sheets containing background data on their fictional concerns. Then the team makes a decision, usually expressed in dollar terms, on the amount of money to be spent on production, marketing, research, or some other area of the concern's business. The impact of these decisions on a mythical market and, consequently, on the other "companies" in the market, is calculated by an umpire, usually a computer programmed with certain cause-and-effect formulas. The umpire changes the situation in accordance with the players' decisions. Reports are issued and then the students, armed with new information, make a new set of decisions, a process that goes on for a predetermined set of "quarters."

Nor is this all. Spicing the game is the requirement that each student-businessman, when he sees that his firm could use a bank loan, travel into nearby Pittsburgh and actually try to talk a local bank out of some cash, fictional though it may be. There, in the plush chambers of bankers such as Francis S. McMichael, vice-president of the Mellon National

Bank and Trust Company, the young applicant haggles, bargains, and negotiates for the desired amount. Later the student is graded in part on how convincingly he made his case.

How complicated games can get, and how wrapped up students can get in them is illustrated by Inter-Nation Simulation, devised in 1958 by a research team headed by Harold Guetzkow, a professor of political science at Northwestern. Developed originally under the auspices of the Carnegie Corporation and the Air Force, the game places participants in the roles of decision makers for make-believe nations. At the same time that the game is supplementing courses in about a dozen universities, Dr. Guetzkow is using it for research, on a $90,000 Defense Department grant.

Dr. Guetzkow explains that players, while working within the limitations of the countries they represent, must attempt to improve their strategic positions in the simulated world arena. Realism is built into the game by requiring the three to five decision makers representing each "country" to concern themselves variously with foreign affairs, domestic economic matters, defense and military problems. One policymaker is vested with overall authority, although all of the players can be deposed from power if they fail to improve the country's standard of living or military strength. This is determined by a set of observers, called "validators," who decide the possible consequences for each nation of decisions made by participants.

Still, decision makers remain free to opt for reduction of political pressures by resorting to international adventures. How the game works in practice was illustrated recently when a group of some thirty Northwestern students in the social sciences participated in 16 three-hour sessions. Unlike students at the Air Force Academy and some other schools that simulate actual nations, the Northwestern participants divided themselves into five mythical lands with varying "histories" and "capabilities." They were Omne and Utro—two relatively strong nations with high productivity rates—and Algo, Erga, and Ingo—three weak nations with limited economic potential.

Professor Guetzkow recalls that the make-believe nations were soon snared in a maelstrom of international tensions. For one thing, both Omne and Utro, through various machinations, grew richer while the economies of the other countries faltered and sputtered. Fueling the uneasiness was the growing military strength of Omne, which alarmed even Utro. Erga called an international conference, ostensibly to discuss economic problems, but in fact to deal with the threat posed by Omne. The poorer countries did glean from the two giants bilateral commitments of economic aid, but they were unable to agree on a strategy to check Omne.

Then Utro rapidly armed, which polarized the "world" system between Omne and Ingo on one side, and Utro and Erga on the other. The only nation without an alliance was Algo, the most impoverished of the five countries. Fearing attack and anxious to carve out a role for itself in the world arena, Algo's policymakers let slip into Ingo's hands a fabricated note, allegedly intercepted from an Erga-Utro courier, revealing plans for an attack on Ingo by the two countries. Ingo immediately called a peace conference, during which Algo offered to act as a mediator between the two blocs. But when tempers flared and tension mounted Algo was forced to admit its authorship of the note. Despite this brinkmanship, peace was maintained; the nations set up a security system that included even Algo. Not all games end so happily. A few, the professor ruefully adds, have ended in nuclear conflagration.

What do students learn from such exercises? Conceding that their value has yet to be proved, Dr. Guetzkow nevertheless insists they are an effective teaching tool. "We put individuals into decision-making posts so they can experience what it's like to operate in an international system," he says. "In a simulated situation students get a sense of the reality of decision making. They learn that it's not as simple as it seems in textbooks."

The students are enthusiastic. After the session, some said they had increased empathy for the plight of small nations in the world arena, while others felt they better understood the phenomenon of nationalism. "I feel like an Omnian," one student confided to an instructor. "In other words, I have developed a nationalist patriotism, pride in Omne's achievements and distress over its failures, which in many ways is just as strong as my American patriotism."

Said another student: "The awareness of the vast number and the complexity of the factors which must be considered by a nation could never have been as vivid from reading a book."

Despite these high marks by students, not all educators are sanguine about games. Indeed, some are downright critical. Discussing the simulation games used by some political scientists, Charles O. Lerche, dean of the school of international services at American University, observes they have "certain advantages in terms of conveying to the student an approximation of reality." But he cautions that the games have "certain built-in limitations. The essence of gaming is that you artificially simplify the universe to single out a few variables. The trouble is that there are few situations in real life where there are only a few variables at work. Life situations are far more complex than these games can make them."

Even on the secondary level not all teachers are enthusiastic about games, which resemble, at least in principle, those played in universities. On both levels games may, but do not always, involve a computer. And even when requiring a computer some games used in high schools seem to border on the frivolous. At least one such game, for example, involves a child's spinning wheel, a pair of dice, and a game board familiar to Monopoly players. Thus the impression persists that games are simply toys, a view that led one Midwest high school last year to turn down a proposal to use in its history classes a seven-year-old politico-military game, called Diplomacy, on grounds that it was "simply entertainment."

Despite such misgivings, use of games on the secondary level is increasing even more rapidly than in the universities. At Johns Hopkins University, James S. Coleman and Sarane

S. Boocock, working under a $200,000 Carnegie Corporation grant, are engaged in the development of games with simulated environments. To these academicians the value of games arises in their ability to "bring the future into the present, allowing the child to play roles in a large, differentiated society of which he otherwise gets hardly a glimpse." Also, they claim, games are peculiarly "self-disciplining" and, finally, "self-judging," meaning "a player knows that he has won or lost by his own actions."

Among the eight exercises so far devised at the school are the Game of Democracy, involving bargaining sessions in which players try to get passed or defeated those measures favored by a make-believe constituency; the Disaster Game, in which the winning player is the one who is most efficient in committing his own energies and most visibly cooperative in helping his neighbors overcome a simulated disaster; and the Consumer Game, involving allocation of income in the face of credit financing and other pressures, in which the player "must learn both economics and mathematics, as well as the necessity to defer gratifications."

One of Johns Hopkins's most widely distributed games is Life Career, in which student teams "play" a hypothetical individual as he moves through life and makes decisions about education, jobs, marriage, and other matters. The team that makes the most realistic decisions, given the qualities of the "individual" whose life they are managing, wins the game. This game proved particularly successful recently when used by some Baltimore high schools to motivate slow-learning students.

Slow learners, in fact, are among the chief beneficiaries of games, say researchers. One game specifically aimed at students considered to be potential dropouts is BMG, developed two years ago by the Western Behavioral Sciences Institute for use in four San Diego schools. Noting that such students are often fond of cars, a WBSI spokesman explains that the young people, for the purpose of the game, play auto manufacturers required to both increase profits and carve out a larger share of the market for their respective "companies." Like some Baltimore and San Diego schools, Nova High School in Ft. Lauderdale also uses games "to meet the educational needs of the student classified as nonmotivated, underachiever, or less capable," says Robert Allen. At the same time, he notes that Nova's games are aimed at "the gifted or advanced student; or the student who has formed negative attitudes about a given subject."

Perhaps more deeply involved in gaming than any other school, Nova now uses about 15 games in its science, mathematics, and social-studies classes. Among them are a smattering of games developed at Johns Hopkins, such as Life Career and the Game of Democracy, and two logic games—Wff'n Proof and Equations—developed by Layman Allen, associate professor of law at Yale University and brother of Nova's Robert Allen.

Such games are by no means used simply as teacher aids, however. During 1965, the first year games were used at Nova, the school divided its mathematics classes into two five-week phases of intramural competition using Wff'n Proof and Equations. Now in its second year, Nova's intramural competition consists of ten leagues, each with anywhere from six to 12 teams. Student gamers push the parallel with athletics about as far as it will go. Each week complete statistics are compiled giving individual and team won-lost records, total points scored, and league standings. Further, teams carry names like The Mods, Rat Finks, Brain Kids, and Clear Thinkers; each week Nova names "a player of the week." Winning teams of the intramural leagues eventually compete in a playoff to determine Nova's representative in the emotion-laden Academic Olympics.

Not surprisingly, some Nova educators worry that such competition may lead to an excessive emphasis on winning rather than learning. But whatever the inherent dangers from such contests, the idea has spread to other school systems. This year

Allegheny County School District near Pittsburgh organized a ten-team interscholastic league around the game Life Career. The contests proved so popular that at one point last fall the young people at one school voted to increase their homework in order to allow more time during the day for playing the game.

Few critics deny that games spur enthusiasm. But they point out that the few studies that have been made fail to confirm that students learn anything from them that could not have been learned from conventional methods. After evaluating the results of six different studies on the educational impact of such exercises as Life Career, Disaster Game, Inter-Nation Simulation, and others, Cleo H. Cherryholmes, a political scientist at Michigan State University, said his findings were disappointing. While agreeing that simulations do create more student motivation and interest, he found that they produce no consistent or significant difference in learning, retention, critical thinking, or attitude change. "Students do not learn significantly more facts or principles by participating in a simulation than in a more conventional classroom activity," he reported recently in the *American Behavioral Scientist*.

Even so, Dr. Cherryholmes allows that it is "plausible to assume that simulations produce effects that have not been specified and measured" in the studies analyzed. He suggests that more attention should be given the "social-psychological impact" of games, and it is precisely in this area that Johns Hopkins's Dr. Boocock insists games can have a profound effect. To prove it she tested the impact of Life Career and the Game of Democracy on some 1,200 4-H Club delegates attending a national conference. Half the young people were plated in an experimental group that played the games while the other half were part of a control group that did not.

She found that participants tended to gain from the legislative game a more realistic view of the pressures on legislators that prevent their acting solely on "principle." Perhaps more important, the "data revealed a trend toward greater feelings of political efficacy" on the part of the players after the exercise. Thus, she believes her findings have significance in the light of several sociological studies of political behavior, which have shown that the people most likely to take an active part in politics are those with strong feelings of "potency" or efficacy. "In other words, the unique contribution of the simulation experience to feelings of efficacy may be in giving young people the confidence needed to *act* upon the intellectual information they have acquired about a political or other social situation," says Dr. Boocock, writing in the *American Behavioral Scientist.*

There is no question that games, when properly used, can have value. When used in conjunction with other materials, they can provide useful points of departure for discussion. At best, then, games can supplement other educational programs, making real and vivid material that often seems abstract in a textbook. If nothing else, they can convey to the player a feeling for the complexity and multiplicity of factors that must be considered in decision making. And conceivably they may increase the confidence of young people to deal with real world problems that seem impossibly remote from their own lives.

But the nature of games makes them vulnerable to abuse, particularly in the hands of inexperienced or lazy teachers. Used in isolation from books or discussion groups, the danger arises that games—most of which mirror political and economic institutions as they are—may encourage quiescent and conformist attitudes. In the course of playing, students may hone techniques that enable them to master the game. One may question whether this spurs critical thinking, since success is premised on accepting the "simulated reality" as it is rather than on examining what is wrong with it.

Equally worrisome is the heavy emphasis often placed on winning, which may mislead the player as to the real objectives of learning. That is, the short-term pressures generated for popular success may lead the player to conclude that the ultimate virtue is simply a workable and, at the same time, rather manipulative strategy. So while gaming may produce an academic hero, doubts remain whether the values underpinning his emergence will be any less superficial than those that have glorified the athlete.

It is, of course, too early to resolve such reservations and, for that matter, too early to be pessimistic about the newfangled exercises. Whatever the uncertainties that now surround games, some things can be said for certain. The burgeoning market for games reflects further movement away from two long-time staples of the classroom: unrealistic and idealized textbook views of American life, and the old teacher-pupil relationship in which the former hands down pronouncements to be regurgitated by the latter. Increasingly the focus is on realism, and increasingly students are expected to learn by themselves. Or at least without the intervention of Gradgrind teachers drilling home facts by slamming rulers on desktops.

XII. So What Do You Do Now?

You ARE A TEACHER in an ordinary school, and the ideas in this book make sense to you . . . what can you do about it, say tomorrow?

1. Your first act of subversion might be conducted in the following way: write on a scrap of paper these questions:

What am I going to have my students do today?
What's it good for?
How do I know?

Tape the paper to the mirror in your bathroom or some other place where you are likely to see it every morning. If nothing else, the questions will begin to make you uneasy about shilling for someone else and might weaken your interest in "following the syllabus." You may even, after a while, become nauseous at the prospect of teaching things which have a specious value or for which there is no evidence that your anticipated outcomes do, in fact, occur. At their best, the questions will drive you to reconsider almost everything you are doing, with the result that you will challenge your principal, your textbooks, the syllabus, the grading system, your own education, and so on. In the end, it all may cost you your job, or lead you to seek another position, or drive you out of teaching altogether. Subversion is a risky business—as risky for its agent as for its target.

2. In class, try to avoid *telling* your students any answers, if only for a few lessons or days. Do not prepare a lesson plan. Instead, confront your students with some sort of problem which might interest them. Then, allow them to work the problem through without your advice or counsel. Your talk should consist of questions directed to particular students, based on remarks made by those students. If a student asks you a question, tell him that you don't know the answer, even if you do. Don't be frightened by the long stretches of silence that might occur. Silence may mean that the students are thinking. Or it may mean that they are growing hostile. The hostility signifies that the students resent the fact that you have shifted the burden of intellectual activity from you to them. Thought is often painful even if you are accustomed to it. If you are not, it can be unbearable.

There are at least two good accounts of what happens when a teacher refrains from telling students answers. One of them appears in Nathaniel Cantor's *The Dynamics of Learning;* the other, in Carl Rogers' *On Becoming a Person.* You may want to read these accounts before trying your experiment. If you have any success at all, you ought to make your experiment a regular feature of your weekly lessons: one hour every day for independent problem solving, or one hour every week. However much you can do will be worth the effort.

3. Try listening to your students for a day or two. We do not mean reacting to what they say. We mean listening. This may require that you do some role playing. Imagine, for example,

that you are not their teacher but a psychiatrist (or some such person) who is not primarily trying to teach but who is trying to understand. Any questions you ask or remarks you make would, therefore, not be designed to instruct or judge. They would be attempts to clarify what someone has said. If you are like most teachers, your training has probably not included learning how to listen. Therefore, we would recommend that you obtain a copy of *On Becoming a Person* by Carl Rogers. The book is a collection of Rogers' best articles and speeches. Rogers is generally thought of as the leading exponent of nondirective counseling, and he is a rich source of ideas about listening to and understanding other people. You probably will not want to read every article in the book, but do not overlook "Communication: Its Blocking and Facilitation." In this article, Rogers describes a particularly effective technique for teaching listening: the students engage in a discussion of some issue about which they have strong feelings. But their discussion has an unusual rule applied to it. A student may say anything he wishes but only after he has restated what the previous speaker has said *to that speaker's satisfaction*. Astounding things happen to students when they go through this experience. They find themselves concentrating on what others are saying to the point, sometimes, of forgetting what they themselves were going to say. In some cases, students have a unique experience. They find that they have projected themselves into the frame of mind of another person. You might wish to make this special listening game a permanent part of your weekly lessons. But, of course, you ought to try it yourself first. An additional aid to you in your efforts at listening will be "Do You Know How to Listen?" by Wendell Johnson. The article apeared in *ETC*. In autumn 1949. This publication is edited by S. I. Hayakawa, and we enthusiastically suggest that you become a permanent subscriber.

It is important for us to say that the principal reason for your learning how to listen to students is that you may increase your understanding of what the students perceive as relevant. The only way to know where a kid is "at" is to listen to what he is saying. You can't do this if you are talking.

Invite another teacher to observe your class when you are experimenting with listening. After the lesson, ask your colleague this question: On the basis of what you heard these students say, what would you have them do tomorrow, or next week? Perhaps your colleague will then invite you to observe her class while she experiments with listening. After a while, both of you may find that you are becoming increasingly more effective at designing activities based on what students actually know, feel, and care about.

If you are somewhat uncertain about how to start your students talking, look back at the chapter "What's Worth Knowing?" Several of the questions listed there will trigger enough student talk to challenge your powers as listener.

4. If you feel it is important for your students to learn how to ask questions, try this:

Announce to the class that for the next two days, you will not permit them to make any utterances that are not in the form of questions. Then, present the class with some problem. Tell them that their task is to compile a list of questions, the answers to which might help in solving the problem. If your students require an inducement, tell them you will reward (with A's, gold stars, or whatever sugar cubes you conventionally use) those students who produce the most questions. At this point, you need only be concerned with the quantity of questions, not their quality. Your students probably have had very little experience with question-asking behavior (at least in school), and the primary problem is to get them to begin formulating questions. Later, you can have them examine their questions in an effort to determine if there are certain criteria by which the quality of a question can be evaluated. (For example: Does the question contain unwarranted assumptions? Does it leave important terms undefined? Does it suggest some procedure for obtaining an answer?)

You might use some such problems as the following, depending on the age of your students:

Suppose we wanted to make the school the best possible school we can imagine, what would you need to know in order to proceed?

Read the following speech (for example, by the President). What would you need to know in order to evaluate the validity of the speech?

Suppose our job was to make recommendations to improve the traffic problem (or pollution problem or population problem or whatever), what would you need to know in order to suggest a solution?

5. In order to help yourself become more aware of the subjectivity of your judgments, try this experiment:

The next time you grade your students, write down your reasons for whatever grade you assigned to a student. Then, imagine that you are the student. Study the reasons that your teacher gave to explain your grade. Ask yourself if you can accept these reasons and reflect on what you think of a teacher who would offer them. You might discover that your basis for assigning grades is prejudicial to some students, or lacks generosity, or is too vague. You might also discover, as some teachers have, that the conventional grading system is totally inadequate to evaluate the learning process. Some teachers have grown to resent it bitterly and have been driven to invent another system to complement the one they are forced to use.

Another experiment that might be helpful: Each time you give a grade to a student, grade your own perception of that student. The following questions might be useful:

1. To what extent does my own background block me from understanding the behavior of this student?

2. Are my own values greatly different from those of the student?

3. To what extent have I made an effort to understand how things look from this student's point of view?

4. To what extent am I rewarding or penalizing the student for his acceptance or rejection of my interests?

5. To what extent am I rewarding a student for merely saying what I want to hear, whether or not he believes or understands what he is saying?

You may discover that your answers to these questions are deeply disturbing. For example, you may find that you give the lowest grades mostly to those students you least understand, in which case, the problem is yours—isn't it?—not theirs. What we are driving at is this: too many teachers seem to believe that the evaluations they make of their students reflect only the "characteristics," "ability," and "behavior" of the students. The teacher merely records the grade that the student "deserves." This is complete nonsense, of course. A grade is as much a product of the teacher's characteristics, ability, and behavior as of the student's. Any procedure you can imagine that would increase your awareness of the role you play in "making" the student what you think he is will be helpful, even something like the following:

Keep track of the judgments you make about students. Every time you *say* words such as right, wrong, good, bad, correct, incorrect, smart, stupid, nice, annoying, polite, impertinent, neat, sloppy, etc., keep a record. Do it yourself or have a student do it. You can simply make a check on a sheet of paper that has been divided in two, with one column marked "+" and the other marked "−." Beyond the verbal judgments, you might keep track of the judgments you make that are made visible nonverbally, through facial expression, gesture, or general demeanor. Negative judgments are, not surprisingly, impediments to good learning, particularly if they have the effect of causing the learner to judge himself negatively.

Positive judgments, perhaps surprisingly, can also produce undesirable results. For example, if a learner becomes totally dependent upon the positive judgments of an authority (teacher) for both motivation and reward, what you have is an intellectual paraplegic incapable of any independent activity, intellectual or otherwise.

The point to all of this is to help you become conscious of the degree to which your language and thought is judgmental. You cannot avoid making judgments but you can become more conscious of the way in which you make them. This is critically important because once we judge someone or something we tend to stop thinking about them or it. Which means, among other things, that we behave in response to our judgments rather than to that which is being judged. People and things are processes. Judgments convert them into fixed states. This is one reason that judgments are commonly self-fulfilling. If a boy, for example, is judged as being "dumb" and a "nonreader" early in his school career, that judgment sets into motion a series of teacher behaviors that cause the judgment to become self-fulfilling.

What we need to do then, if we are seriously interested in helping students to become good learners, is to suspend or delay judgments about them. One manifestation of this is the ungraded elementary school. But you can practice suspending judgment yourself tomorrow. It doesn't require any major changes in anything in the school except your own behavior.

For example, the following incident—in this case outside of a classroom—is representative of the difference between a stereotypic and a suspended judgment.

A man and his seventeen-year-old son on Monday evening had a "discussion" about the need for the son to defer his social activities on week nights until he has finished doing all of the home work he has for school the next day.

It is now Wednesday evening, 48 hours later, about 7:30 P.M.

Father is watching TV. Son emerges from his room and begins to put on a jacket.

FATHER: Where are you going?
SON: Out.
FATHER: Out where?
SON: Just out.
FATHER: Have you finished your home work?
SON: Not yet.
FATHER: I thought we decided [that's the way parents talk]

that you wouldn't go out on week nights until you'd finished your home work.

SON: But I have to go out.

FATHER: What do you mean you "have to"?

SON: I just do.

FATHER: Well, you're not going out. You just have to learn to live up to the terms of the agreements you make.

SON: But . . .

FATHER: That's all. I want no back talk.

MOTHER: Please. Let him go out. He'll be back soon.

FATHER: I don't want you butting in.

MOTHER [to son]: Go ahead. It will be all right.

[Son exits.]

FATHER [in a rage]: What the hell do you mean by encouraging his impertinence. How do you expect him to learn responsibility if you side with him in an argument with me? How . . .

MOTHER [interrupting]: Do you know what tomorrow is?

FATHER: What the hell has that got to do with it? Tomorrow's Thursday.

MOTHER: Yes, and it's your birthday.

FATHER: [Silence.]

MOTHER: Your son has been making a birthday gift for you at Jack's house. He wanted it to be a surprise for you tomorrow morning. A nice start for the day. He has just a bit more work to do on it to finish it. He wanted to get it done as early as possible tonight so he could bring it home and wrap it up for tomorrow. And then he'd still have time to do his home work.

Well, you see how easy it is to judge someone as something on the basis of x amount of data perceived in one way while simultaneously they are not only not that, but are something quite different.

Judgments are relative to the data upon which they are based and to the emotional state of the judge.

Learning to suspend judgment can be most liberating. You might find that it makes you a better learner (meaning maker) too.

6. Along the lines of the above, we would suggest an experiment that requires only imagination, but plenty of it. Suppose you could convince yourself that your students are the smartest children in the school; or, if that seems unrealistic, that they have the greatest potential of any class in the school. (After all, who can say for certain how much potential anyone has?) What do you imagine would happen? What would you do differently if you *acted* as if your students were capable of great achievements? And if you acted differently, what are the chances that many of your students would begin to act as if they *were* great achievers? We believe that the chances are quite good. There is, as we have noted, considerable evidence to indicate that people can become what others think they are. In fact, if you reflect on how anyone becomes anything, you are likely to conclude that becoming is almost always a product of expectations—one's own or someone else's. We are talking here about the concept of the "self-fulfilling prophecy." This refers to the fact that often when we predict that something will happen, the prediction itself contributes to making it happen. Nowhere is this idea more usable than in education, which is, or ought to be, concerned with the processes of becoming.

A *warning:* you will have great difficulty in imagining that your students are smart if you hold on to the belief that the stuff you know about, or would like to know about, constitutes the only ingredients of "smartness." Once you abandon that idea, you may find that your students do, in fact, know a great deal of stuff, and that it is easier than you supposed to imagine they are the brightest children you ever had.

7. The extent to which you can try the following experiment depends on the degree to which the administration and the school community are rigid. In its most effective form, the experiment involves telling your students that all of them will get A's for the term and, of course, making good on your promise. At first, the students will not believe you, and it has sometimes taken as long as four weeks before all the students accept the situation. Once such acceptance is achieved, the

students can begin to concentrate on learning, not their grades. There is no need for them to ask, "When is the midterm?" "Do we have to do a paper?" "How much weight is given to classwork?" and so on. If such questions do arise, you can reply, honestly, by saying that the questions are not necessary since the grades have already been given and each student will receive the highest possible grade the system allows. (We can assure you that such questions will come up because students have been conditioned to think of education as being indistinguishable from grades.) The next step is to help the students discover what kind of knowledge they think is worth knowing and to help them decide what procedures can most profitably be used to find out what they want to know. You will have to remind your students that there is no need for them to make suggestions that they think will please *you*. Neither is there any need for them to accept your suggestions out of fear of reprisal. Once they internalize this idea, they will pursue vigorously whatever course their sense of relevance dictates. Incidentally, they are likely to view your proposals not as threats, but as possibilities. In fact, you may be astonished at how seriously your own suggestions are regarded once the coercive dimension is removed.

If you are thinking that students, given such conditions, will not do any work, you are wrong. Most will. But, of course, not all. There are always a few who will view the situation as an opportunity to "goof off." So what? It is a small price to pay for providing the others with perhaps the only decent intellectual experience they will ever have in school. Beyond that, the number of students who do "goof off" is relatively small when compared with those who, in conventional school environments, tune out.

There is no way of our predicting what "syllabus" your students will evolve. It depends. Especially on them, but also on you and how willing you are to permit students to take control of the direction of their own studies. If you, or your administration and community, could not bear this possibility, perhaps you could try the experiment on a limited basis: for example, for a "unit" or even a specific assignment.

8. Perhaps you have noticed that most examinations and, indeed, syllabi and curricula deal almost exclusively with the past. The future hardly exists in school. Can you remember ever asking or being asked in school a question like "If such and such occurs, what do you think *will* happen?"? A question of this type is usually not regarded as "serious" and would rarely play a central role in any "serious" examination. When a future-oriented question is introduced in school, its purpose is usually to "motivate" or to find out how "creative" the students can be. But the point is that the world we live in is changing so rapidly that a future-orientation is essential for everybody. Its development in schools is our best insurance against a generation of "future shock" sufferers.

You can help by including in all of your class discussions and examinations some questions that deal with the future. For example:

What effects on our society do you think the following technological inventions will have?
a. the electric car
b. the television-telephone
c. the laser beam
d. the 2,000-mph jet
e. central data storage
f. disposable "paper" clothing
g. interplanetary communication
h. language-translation machines
Can you identify two or three ideas, beliefs, and practices that human beings will need to give up for their future well-being?

In case you are thinking that such questions as these are usable only in the higher grades, we want to assure you that young children (even third-graders) frequently provide imaginative and pointed answers to future-oriented questions, provided that the questions are suitably adapted to their level of understanding. Perhaps you can make it a practice to include future-oriented questions at least once a week in all your classes. It is especially important that this be done for young children. After all, by the time they have finished school, the future you have asked them to think about will be the present.

9. Anyone interested in helping students deal with the future (not to mention the present) would naturally be concerned, even preoccupied, with media of communication. We recommend to you, of course, the books of Marshall McLuhan, especially *Understanding Media*. We think that the most productive way to respond to McLuhan's challenge (as he has suggested) is *not* to examine his statements but to examine the media. In other words, don't dwell on the question "Is McLuhan right in saying such and such?" Instead, focus on the question "In what ways are media affecting our society?" Your answers may turn out to be better than McLuhan's. More important, if you allow your students to consider the question, *their* answers may be better than McLuhan's. And even more important than that, the process of searching for such answers, once learned, will be valuable to your students throughout their lives.

Therefore, we suggest that media study become an integral part of all your classes. No matter what "subject" you are teaching, media are relevant. For example, if you are a history teacher, you can properly consider questions about the effects of media on political and social developments. If you are a science teacher, the entire realm of technology is open to you and your students, including a consideration of the extent to which technology influences the direction of the evolutionary process. If you are an English teacher, the role of media in creating new literatures, new audiences for literature, and new modes of perceiving literature is entirely within your province. In short, regardless of your subject and the age of your students, we suggest that you include the study of media as a normal part of the curriculum. You might bear in mind that your students are quite likely to be more perceptive and even more knowledgeable about the structure and meaning of newer media than you. For example, there are many teachers who haven't yet noticed that young people are enormously interested in poetry—the poetry that is now on LP records and sung by Joan Baez, Phil Ochs, and Bob Dylan; or that young people are equally interested in essays of social and political criticism—as *heard* on records by Lenny Bruce, Bill Cosby, Godfrey Cambridge, Mort Sahl, et al.

10. Before making our final suggestion, we want to say a word of assurance about the revolution we are urging. There is nothing in what we have said in this book that precludes the use, *at one time or another*, of any of the conventional methods and materials of learning. For certain specific purposes, a lecture, a film, a textbook, a packaged unit, even a punishment, may be entirely justified. What we are asking for is a methodological and psychological shift in emphasis in the roles of teacher and student, a fundamental change in the *nature* of the classroom environment. In fact, one model for such an environment already exists in the schools—oddly, at the extreme ends of the schooling process. A good primary-grade teacher as well as a good graduate-student adviser operate largely on the subversive assumptions expressed in this book. They share a concern for process as against product. They are learner- and problem-oriented. They share a certain disdain for syllabi. They allow their students to pursue that which is relevant to the learner. But there is a 15-year gap between the second grade and advanced graduate study. The gap can be filled, we believe, by teachers who understand the spirit of our orientation. It is neither required nor desirable that *everything* about one's performance as a teacher be changed. Just the most important things.

11. Our last suggestion is perhaps the most difficult. It requires honest self-examination. Ask yourself how you came to know whatever things you feel are worth knowing. This may sound like a rather abstract inquiry, but when undertaken seriously it frequently results in startling discoveries. For example, some teachers have discovered that there is almost nothing valuable they know that was *told* to them by someone

else. Other teachers have discovered that their most valuable knowledge was *not* learned in a recognizable sequence. Still others begin to question the meaning of the phrase "valuable knowledge" and wonder if anything they learned in school was "valuable." Such self-examination can be most unsettling, as you can well imagine. English teachers have discovered that they hate Shakespeare; history teachers, that everything they know about the Wars of the Roses is useless; science teachers, that they really wanted to be druggists. The process, once begun, leads in many unexpected directions but most often to the question "Why am I a teacher, anyway?" Some honest answers that this question has produced are as follows:

> I can control people.
> I can tyrannize people.
> I have captive audiences.
> I have my summers off.
> I love seventeenth-century nondramatic Elizabethan literature.
> I don't know.
> The pay is good, considering the amount of work I actually do.

Obviously, none of these answers is very promising for the future of our children. But each in its way is a small act of positive subversion because it represents a teacher's honest attempt to know himself. The teacher who *recognizes* that he is interested, say, in exercising tyrannical control over others is taking a first step toward subverting that interest. But the question "Why am I a teacher, anyway?" also produces answers that are encouraging: for example, that one can participate in the making of intelligence and, thereby, in the development of a decent society. As soon as a teacher recognizes that this is, in fact, the reason he became a teacher, then the subversion of our existing educational system strikes him as a necessity. As we have been trying to say: we agree.

XIII. Strategies for Survival

> We have modified our environment so radically
> that we must now modify ourselves in order to
> exist in this new environment.
> —NORBERT WIENER, *The Human Use
> of Human Beings*

THE BASIC FUNCTION of all education, even in the most traditional sense, is to increase the survival prospects of the group.
If this function is fulfilled, the group survives. If not, it doesn't.
There have been times when this function was not fulfilled,
and groups (some of them we even call "civilizations") disappeared. Generally, this resulted from changes in the kinds
of threats the group faced. The threats changed, but the education did not, and so the group, in a way, "disappeared itself"
(to use a phrase from *Catch-22*). The tendency seems to be
for most "educational" systems, from patterns of training in
"primitive" tribal societies to school systems in technological
societies, to fall imperceptibly into a role devoted exclusively
to the conservation of old ideas, concepts, attitudes, skills, and

perceptions. This happens largely because of the unconsciously held belief that these old ways of thinking and doing are necessary to the survival of the group. And that is largely true, IF the group inhabits an environment in which change occurs very, very slowly, or not at all. Survival in a stable environment depends almost entirely on remembering the strategies for survival that have been developed in the past, and so the conservation and transmission of these becomes the primary mission of education. But, a paradoxical situation develops when change becomes the primary characteristic of the environment. Then the task turns inside out—survival in a rapidly changing environment depends almost entirely upon being able to identify which of the old concepts are relevant to the demands imposed by the new threats to survival, and which are not. Then a new educational task becomes critical: getting the group to unlearn (to "forget") the irrelevant concepts as a prior condition to learning. What we are saying is that "selective forgetting" is necessary to survival.

We suggest that this is the stage we have now reached environmentally, and so we must now work to reach this stage educationally. The only thing that is at stake is our survival.

It is not possible to overstate the fact that technologically wrought changes in the environment render virtually all of our traditional concepts (survival strategies)—and the institutions developed to conserve and transmit them—irrelevant, but not merely irrelevant. If we fail to detect the fact that they are irrelevant, these concepts themselves become threats to our survival.

This idea is not, of course, original with us, even though it is new. It is new because up until just recently changes in the environment did not require it. As might be expected, the idea was first articulated by those most familiar with and concerned about technologically produced change—scientists. Not all scientists to be sure, since not all scientists themselves have been able to unlearn irrelevant old concepts. After all, science is itself so new that 95 percent of all the scientists who ever lived are alive right now!

Examples of the kinds of institutional and conceptual change that we are talking about, even outside of science, are not hard to find, even though the degree to which this kind of change is occurring is much less than environmental change requires. The Ecumenical Council, convened by Pope John XXIII, is one illustration of several kinds of changes occurring in the form and substance of theological institutions. These changes are occurring, of course, in response to radical environmental changes. During the Ecumenical Council, several major changes in traditional concepts—as well as in the forms in which they have been taught, including many that had been conserved for almost 2,000 years—were "selectively forgotten." Some of them, such as the unlearning of the concept that "Christ was killed by the Jews," seemed ludicrously belated In the interests of its own survival, however, the Church made these changes. Pope John saw that the Council was necessary to "close the gap" between the conceptual and formal structure of the Church as an institution and new environmental demands upon its constituency. The gap between the Church and its constituents was a product of the fact that change was occurring in the environment outside the Church, but not inside. As a result, the membership of the Church was disappearing. In order to avoid disappearing itself, the Church had to change in ways that were perceived as relevant to its potential constituency. Note that the concept "God is dead" is under serious discussion in theological circles today, clearly indicating that the old concept of God itself is undergoing a change.

One "concept" that is still at issue is that of "contraception" (along with "abortion"). The sanctions against "birth control" were probably "reasonable" while environmental threats to survival included certain facts of physical mortality. Those "facts" are no longer operational because technological "progress" has virtually eliminated them. This is one "concept" that has to turn "inside out" because change has turned the facts of the environment "inside out." Now we are at the point where the uncontrolled proliferation of human life itself (the population explosion) is a threat—and a totally unprecedented one—to our survival.

More immediately in our own society, the theologically related legal concept of abortion is undergoing "selective forgetting" or unlearning in the form of the repeal of laws against it.

Almost all of the concepts that we have had—painfully—to unlearn as a group resulted (and are resulting) from the use of scientific method. When Galileo, using scientific method, suggested that Western man would have to unlearn the concept that he was the center of the universe, the institutions devoted to the conservation and transmission of this concept responded with something less than enthusiasm. Galileo had the choice of shutting up about this "subversive" new concept or being shut up. He was scientific enough to figure out that he wouldn't be able to say anything if he were dead. In this respect he was rather different from some of our contemporaries who begin statements with the phrase "Better dead . . ." The concept that it is better to be dead is a curious one for anyone to hold who is ostensibly concerned with survival.

Along similar lines, to cite another illustration of our point, when Charles Darwin, again employing the method of science, made certain observations with his naked eye (Galileo had used an "unholy" instrument consisting of a tube with lenses in it) that led him to suggest that the concept of the origin of man depicted in Genesis might require unlearning, the institutions committed to the conservation and transmission of this concept were, again, less than delighted. The response to Darwin, however, was quantitatively different (the Scopes trial notwithstanding) from that to Galileo. A number of cracks in "concept monopoly" had developed between Galileo and Darwin (with the printing press not being the least of these), so Darwin did find some support (mostly among scientists), whereas Galileo did not. One of the hazards of being first is that you leave everyone else behind.

We must emphasize that the concept "that we must unlearn

dead concepts" is itself new, and so rather uncongenial to most who confront it for the first time.

To date, a great deal of human energy has been spent on the search for the "holy grail" of the illusion of certainty. As a group, we are still in our intellectual infancy, depending much more upon magic and superstition than upon reason to allay our anxieties about the universe in which we are trying to live. After all, we haven't had much practice at figuring things out scientifically. So far, the use of scientific method is still largely confined to producing things nominally intended to increase physical comfort. Up until just recently, technological "progress" has been confined almost solely to extending and shifting the function of human physical strength and energy to machines with which we cannot now compete. And while we have yet to figure out solutions to the problems this elementary kind of "progress" has produced, we are just beginning to confront the problems emerging as a consequence of the assumption by electronic machines of human intellectual functions. Electronic machines just happen to perform—already—a range of intellectual tasks better than human beings can. Our space-probing program, for example, would simply not be possible without electronic extensions of human information-handling and decision-making functions. The environmental changes electronic machines will produce in the near future—if not in the immediate present—is the subject of serious concern and discussion right now. One such discussion, accessible to a large public audience via television, occurred on the NBC *Open Mind* program. The participants were Paul Armer, associate head of the Rand Corporation's Computer Science Department, Theodore Kheel, Secretary-Treasurer of the American Foundation on Automation and Employment, Charles De Carlo, Director of Automation Research at I.B.M., and Robert Theobald, consulting economist and author of *The Challenge of Abundance.*

Threaded throughout the expert estimates of actual and imminent changes were references to the educational tasks to be fulfilled if these changes are not to disrupt the society in which they are occurring and will increasingly occur.

Robert Theobald, focusing on education, restated the sense of the discussion by saying that incredible changes are going to take place within 35 years and that no human group has ever before faced the problem of coping with changes of such magnitude. Noting that cultures have failed because they were incapable of changing their old concepts and ways of thinking, he suggested that we have to help the young people in our culture learn a new set of beliefs, a new set of institutions, and a new set of values, which will allow them to live in a totally different world. The issue, he said, lies here: how do you change the thinking of a culture with enormous speed?

Our response is that you do it through the school system—which is the only social institution that exists to fulfill this function—and by explicitly helping students to internalize concepts relevant to new environmental demands. Theobald, emphasizing that this is not a hypothetical problem and synthesizing the sense of the remarks of other participants, made the point that as a culture we have yet to see and understand the changes that have already taken place much less those that are about to. He noted also that the term "future shock" is coming into currency.

Clearly, there is no more important function for education to fulfill than that of helping us to recognize the world we actually live in and, simultaneously, of helping us to master concepts that will increase our ability to cope with it. This is the essential criterion for judging the relevance of all education.

Harold G. Shane, in "Future Shock and the Curriculum" (*Phi Delta Kappan*, October 1967), documents the sources and significance of this new educational task and suggests why it is new:

> The possible consequences of future shock for education are considerable. Let us first review the sources of the dislocation

that seems to threaten the composure and effectiveness of individuals involved in educational leadership, research, and service.

During the 1920s and 1930s the educational scene in the U.S. was a lively one. Changes were made in methods and materials, and periodical literature was full of stimulating ideas. Manuscript writing, the project method, teacher-pupil planning, social reconstruction through education, and a hundred similar proposals found strident supporters and dogged opponents.

Violent as the debates of the times became, however, no one seemed to be traumatized or even seriously upset as verbal warfare between conservative and liberal, between "subject-oriented" and "learner-oriented," forces enlivened commerce in the free market of educational ideas. Certainly, prior to the 1950s there was less uneasiness, less uncertainty, and less poorly concealed panic about the nature, the merit, and the speed of educational change than there is now.

No real future shock was experienced by educators of this era because new practices—despite the debates they generated—were rarely rapid and generally were *extensions* and *refinements* of familiar ideas, methods, and procedures rather than basic *changes* or *innovations* involving heretofore unfamiliar technologies or based on concepts with little or no precedent.

What, then, has recently happened *in* education and *to* education to bring on the "dizzying disorientation" caused by a premature collision with the future? Since around 1950 many educators have found themselves confronting new educational directions to which their past learning and experience simply do not transfer.

A decade earlier, Lynn White, Jr. (*Frontiers of Knowledge*, New York: Harper and Bros., 1956) summed up the probable meaning of the newest knowledge of that time under the title "Changing Canons of Culture." Possibly illustrating the rate at which change is occurring, White's views now seem much more sanguine than the state of our schools would seem to permit.

In general, he suggested that seven major "canons" (as he called them) of culture had in fact changed, or had begun to change, as a consequence of activity on the "frontiers of knowledge." Here is how he put it:

> Since the days of the Greeks our thinking has been framed within *the canon of the Occident*. This is the unexamined assumption that civilization par exellence is that of the Western tradition. . . . Our image of the person is ceasing to assume tacitly that the white man is made peculiarly in the likeness of God. [p. 302]
>
> The canon of the Occident has been displaced by *the canon of the globe*. . . . Few of us realize the extent to which our most ordinary actions and thoughts are being formed according to non-Occidental models. [p. 303]
>
> A second major canon which we inherited from the Greeks: *the canon of logic and language*. For more than two thousand years in the West it has been axiomatic that logic and language are perfected instruments of intellectual analysis and expression. . . . Much of our present discussion of education is still based on the premise that the mind which has mastered logic and language is able to achieve clear and efficient results in any field.
>
> But there is a new and more complex canon today, one which does not deny the validity of the canon of logic and language but which puts it into a wider context, just as the canon of the globe does not negate the canon of the Occident but changes its nature by amplifying it.
>
> This second new canon is *the canon of symbols*. . . . We are beginning to see that the distinctive thing about the human species is that we are a symbol-making animal. [p. 305]
>
> Even the way our senses report experience to us may be structured by the conventions of language, art, or the like [add new media]. [p. 306]
>
> A most important aspect of the canon of symbols, therefore, is our realization that while symbols are created by us, these creatures in a peculiar way come alive, turn upon us, and coerce us and our experience to conform to the anatomy. [p. 307]
>
> From the Greeks, again, we inherit *the canon of rationality*, which assumes that reason is the supreme human attribute and that anything other than rationality is "less" than rationality and to be deplored as subhuman. . . .

But we now dwell in a world dominated by *the canon of the unconscious*. Closer scrutiny has shown that a vast lot is happening in the shadowy iridescence, the black opal of the abyss which lies within each of us. [p. 308]

The realization of the scope, the dangers, and the potentialities of the unconscious is essential to our new image of the person.

It is significant that, more and more, we are using the word *unconscious* rather than *subconscious*. The latter is involved in metaphorical association of up-and-down spatial relationships with value judgments, and it thus might trick us into assuming that the unconscious is in some way *sub* and therefore inferior or unworthy. This aspect of the new canon of the unconscious illustrates the fourth, and final, major change of canon which is observable in our culture.

. . . Ever since the great days of Athens we have generally thought, felt, and acted in terms of *the canon of the hierarchy of values*. We have assumed and consciously taught that some types of human activity are more worthy of study and reverence than others because the contemplation of them seemed to bring greater spiritual rewards. This hierarchy of values, expressed most clearly in the ancient concept of the liberal arts, was codified in the Middle Ages, expanded in the Renaissance and post-Renaissance, and has continued to be manifest in emphasis on the importance of mathematics, logic, philosophy, literature, and the unapplied sciences. [p. 310]

The Greeks and Romans, . . . living in a slave economy, considered use of the hands . . . contemptible. [p. 311]

The old canon of the hierarchy or ladder of values has turned at right angles to become a *new canon of the spectrum of values*. Whereas the old canon insisted that some human activities are by their nature more intellectually and spiritually profitable than others, the new canon holds that every human activity, whether changing diapers or reading Spinoza, whether plowing for barley or measuring galaxies, enshrines the possibility—perhaps not the actuality but the potentiality—of greatness: its proper contemplation and practice promise the reward of insight. . . . Just as the economic and political revolutions of our time have produced an egalitarian society, so our intellectual revolution has insisted on—what would have seemed a logical and semantic absurdity to former ages—an equality of values. Indeed, we suddenly realize the weakness of our verbal symbols: clearly "value" is a monetary metaphor, inherently scaled up-and-down rather than sideways. Yet we have no other serviceable word, so we must use the term "value," understanding in what sense it is obsolete. [p. 312]

All four of the old canons which have suffered a sea change in the storms of our time were formulated by the first consciously Occidental society, that of Athens. In the realm of thought and emotion, twenty-four centuries of Hellenic dominance now are ended. The marvel is not that our vision is confused but rather that we are learning so quickly how to view mankind from vantage-points other than the Acropolis. [p. 313]

Practically every book we read, every speech we hear, every TV show or moving picture we see, every conversation around us is formulated and phrased, at least on the surface, in terms of the old canons of the Occident, of logic and language, or rationality and of the hierarchy of values. This outer form, however, is a violation of the inner substance. In theological terms, our culture has experienced a transubstantiation and it is our spiritual task to recognize the actualities and not be deceived by the accidents. It would be useful as an intellectual discipline to apply to our analysis of what goes on about us the four new canons of the globe, of symbols, of the unconscious, and of the spectrum of values. Since each of them is no more than a cultural reflection of a changed concept of what a human being is, these canons may help us to understand not only our age but ourselves. [p. 316]

If, as he wrote, White had thoughtfully looked at the schools, he would have found that they were deeply devoted to the job of "inculcating" the old canons he said had changed. Anyone who looks at the schools today will find them *still* "inculcating" the old canons. The schools stare fixedly into the past as we hurtle pell-mell into the future.

Not only are the archaic canons—or concepts—White hopefully suggested had changed still being "taught," but so are a series of other equally out-of-joint concepts, some deriving from those he noted. Among the more obvious of these are the following:

1. The concept of absolute, fixed, unchanging "truth," particularly from a polarizing good-bad perspective.

2. The concept of certainty. There is always one and only one "right" answer, and it is absolutely "right."

3. The concept of isolated identity, that "A is A" period, simply, once and for all.

4. The concept of fixed states and "things," with the implicit concept that if you know the name you understand the "thing."

5. The concept of simple, single, mechanical causality; the idea that every effect is the result of a single, easily identifiable cause.

6. The concept that differences exist *only* in parallel and opposing forms: good-bad, right-wrong, yes-no, short-long, up-down, etc.

7. The concept that knowledge is "given," that it emanates from a higher authority, and that it is to be accepted without question.

This list is not exhaustive, but, alas, it is representative. What difference does it make—now and in the future—whether students internalize these concepts? What kind of people are they as a result? Here we move to what might be called the "nonintellectual" level of attitudes rather than concepts.

Most criticism of the old education, and the old concepts it conserves and transmits, from Paul Goodman to John Gardner, makes the point that the students who endure it come out as passive, acquiescent, dogmatic, intolerant, authoritarian, inflexible, conservative personalities who desperately need to resist change in an effort to keep their illusion of certainty intact.

It would be difficult to imagine any kind of education less liable to help students to be able to meet a drastically changing future than one which fosters the development of concepts and attitudes such as those noted above.

The concepts that we must all learn—that are now the *raison d'être* of education—are those which both shape technological change and derive from it: they are characteristics of the spirit, mood, language, and process of science. They are operative wherever evidence of social change—including theological versions—can be found.

Some of them you may recognize, and perhaps even accept, at least in certain domains. Others may seem odd or obscure, indicating their, to date, "fugitive" status.

Intellectual strategies for nuclear-space-age survival—in all dimensions of human activity—include such concepts as relativity, probability, contingency, uncertainty, function, structure as process, multiple causality (or noncausality), nonsymmetrical relationships, degrees of difference, and incongruity (or simultaneously appropriate difference).

Concepts such as these, as well as others both implicit in and contingent upon them, comprise the ingredients for changing ourselves in ways that complement the environmental demands that we all must face. The learning of such concepts will produce the kinds of people we will need to deal effectively with a future full of drastic change.

The new education has as its purpose the development of a new kind of person, one who—as a result of internalizing a different series of concepts—is an actively inquiring, flexible, creative, innovative, tolerant, liberal personality who can face uncertainty and ambiguity without disorientation, who can formulate viable new meanings to meet changes in the environment which threaten individual and mutual survival.

The new education, in sum, is new because it consists of having students use the concepts most appropriate to the world in which we all must live. All of these concepts constitute the dynamics of the questing-questioning, meaning-making process that can be called "learning how to learn." This comprises a posture of stability from which to deal fruitfully with change. The purpose is to help all students develop built-in, shockproof crap detectors as basic equipment in their survival kits.

ACKNOWLEDGMENTS

"What Did You Learn in School Today?": words and music by Tom Paxton. © Copyright 1962, 1964, 1965 by Cherry Lane Music, Inc. Used by permission. All rights reserved. Used by permission of Harmony Music Ltd., controlling publisher for the British Commonwealth (excluding Canada) ·and the Republics of Ireland and South Africa. Copyright 1966 for Scandinavia, Finland and Iceland: Musikproduktion Winckler, Copenhagen NV, Denmark.

Review by Raymond W. Arnold: Reprinted by permission of Raymond W. Arnold and New York State Education.

Excerpts from LET US NOW PRAISE FAMOUS MEN by James Agee and Walker Evans: Used by permission of Houghton Mifflin Company.

"The Cheating Scandal: Four Boys on the Carpet": Reprinted by permission of The New York Post. © 1967, New York Post Corporation.

"Education on the Non-Verbal Level" by Aldous Huxley: Reprinted with permission of Daedalus, Journal of the American Academy of Arts and Sciences, Boston, Mass. Spring 1962 "Science & Technology in a Contemporary Society."

Excerpt from THE WAY OF ZEN by Alan Watts: © 1957 by Pantheon Books, Inc. Reprinted by permission of Random House, Inc.

Excerpt from MY LANGUAGE IS ME by Beulah Parker: Used by permission of Basic Books, Inc., Publishers. New York, 1962.

"Teachers Scored by Youth Panel: Lack of Communication Is Called Crux of Problem by 10 Teenagers": © 1967 by The New York Times Company. Reprinted by permission.

"We Need a New Picture of Knowledge" by Marshall McLuhan: Reprinted with permission of the Association for Supervision and Curriculum Development and Marshall McLuhan. Copyright © 1963 by the Association for Supervision and Curriculum Development.

"Education and Reality" by Frank Miceli: Used by permission of the author.

"Games in the Classroom" by Elliott Carlson. Originally published in Saturday Review, April 15, 1967. Used by permission of Saturday Review and the author.

"Students Demand College Reform" by Steven V. Roberts: © 1967 by The New York Times Company. Reprinted by permission.

"Future Shock and the Curriculum" by Harold G. Shane. Originally published in Phi Delta Kappan, October 1967. Used by permission of Phi Delta Kappa and the author.

Abridgment of "The Changing Canons of Our Culture": From FRONTIERS OF KNOWLEDGE edited by Lynn White, Jr. Copyright © 1956 by Harper & Row, Publishers, Incorporated. Used by permission of the publishers.